REPACKAGE
&
GROW RICH

Your new business plan that will guide you toward success and financial freedom

Notice of Rights

All rights reserved. No part of this book may be reproduced or transmitted in any form by any means, electronic, mechanical, photocopying, recording, or otherwise, without the publisher's prior written permission. For information on getting permits for reprints and excerpts, contact info@intellifields.com.

Notice of Liability

The information in this book is distributed on an "As Is" basis, without warranty. While every precaution has been taken in the book's preparation, neither the author nor Intellifields shall have any liability to any person or entity concerning any loss or damage caused or alleged to be caused directly or indirectly by the instructions contained in this book.

Trademarks

All product names and services identified throughout this book are used in editorial fashion only and for the benefit of owner companies with no intention of infringement of the trademark. No such use, or the use of any trade name, is intended to convey endorsement or other affiliation with this book.

For my loving wife, Rasha
You are the star that always guides me.
- Mohamed A. Kamar

TABLE OF CONTENTS

PREFACE 7
INTRODUCTION 11
PART 1 26
    WHY REPACKAGING? 27
    TYPE OF GOODS 35
        COMMODITIES (NEEDS) 35
        NICHE (WANTS) 36
    BLOCK FLOW DIAGRAM 43
    PRE-EXECUTION WORKS 44
        SELECTING YOUR PRODUCT 44
        GATHER INFORMATION 64
        ASSESS YOUR CAPABILITIES 67
    EXECUTION PLAN 70
        PROJECT PHASE 70
        OPERATION PHASE 76
    ACTUAL EXECUTION 77
        BRANDING (PROJECT PHASE) 77
        SELECTING THE PROPER PACKAGE (PROJECT PHASE) 79
        LABEL DESIGN (PROJECT PHASE) 80
        START PROTOTYPING (PRE-OPERATION) 84
        START MARKETING AND SELLING (OPERATION PHASE) .. 89
    BUSINESS STRATEGIES AND SHORTCUTS 93
        OUTSOURCING 93
        PARTNERSHIP 93
        OPM & OPT LEVERAGES 95
    CASE STUDY 101
PART 2 104
    SAVE A LITTLE MONEY FOR A RAINY DAY 105
    DON'T CONFORM TO THE STATUS QUO 108
    PUSHING BEYOND THE BOUNDARIES 110
    STOP PROCRASTINATION 113

PROVIDE VALUE	115
BE THE FIRST ONE IN THE MARKET PLACE	117
INTRODUCE SOMETHING NOVEL	118
GATHER OPINIONS	121
IF YOU ARE LOOKING FOR SECURITY...	123
BOOTSTRAPPING	125
THE POOR, THE MIDDLE CLASS AND THE RICH	127
DIVERSIFY	134
SEARCH FOR A MENTOR	136
SETTING GOALS	138
WHAT YOU THINK ABOUT YOU BRING ABOUT	142
WATCHOUT THE VIBES	144
YOUR FRIENDS	147
IT IS NEVER TOO LATE	149
IMPACT	151
ACHIEVEMENT	153
BREAKDOWN LARGE PROJECTS TO SMALL MANAGEABLE ONE	155
GIVING OFF FOR CHARITY	158
SEARCH FOR PROBLEMS & SOLVE THEM	159
READ	163
CUSTOMER IS KING	165
VALUE OF TIME	167
CLINGING TO LOSS	172
DELAY THE GRATIFICATION	174
TAKE ADVANTAGE OF YOUR APTITUDES	177
WAKE UP EARLY	179
THINK BIG	181
PROTECT YOUR INTELLECTUAL PROPERTY	184
THE IMPORTANCE OF RELATIVE FREEDOM	186
PERSISTENCE AND CONSISTENCY	187
SPEED UP THE PROCESS	189

- WHAT MATTERS MOST IN YOUR LIFE? 191
- THE POWER OF HABITS 193
- FEAR OF FAILURE 196
- EDUCATION 197
- FOCUS YOUR GOALS 199
- NEVER GIVE UP 201

CONCLUSION 203
RECOMMENDED READINGS...204
APPENDIX 1 205
APPENDIX 2 222
APPENDIX 3 232
APPENDIX 4 242

PREFACE

"In peace, prepare for war. In war, prepare for peace."
Sun Tzu (the art of war)

If you are an employee who is looking for owning your own business or a retiree who is looking for investing in the right place to secure your future life or even a business owner who is looking to improving your own business. Then, this book is for you.

We studied business during our school and college years, but we were taught all that is required to make the other guy rich. We did not explore how to build businesses from scratch. We did not know that by owning even a small kiosk down a street corner, we are considered to be an entrepreneur.

"When you say 'follow me on Twitter,' and you get 10 million people to follow you - you just leveraged your influence to add value to an app that you have no ownership in".
Nipsey Hussle

That's how ultra-rich people become rich; they use other people's talents and resources and only compensate them with peanuts for their hard work.

No one taught us that to be a successful businessman, you have to handle rejection. No one taught us that you have to fall and stand up very quickly to show yourself first, your beloved ones, and the entire world that you won't give up easily.

> "I have not failed. I've just found 10,000 ways that won't work."
> Thomas A. Edison

So is this another book on how to get rich quick that you are going to read and won't gain anything tangible? The answer is no; This book is different. It is different because it includes simple guidelines to start a successful business by proposing realistic schemes and not relying on just inspiration and motivation. Of course, there is nothing wrong with inspiration and motivation, but you cannot solely rely on them to get rich; otherwise, we would have stayed at home meditating all days long.

Book stores have many "How to get rich quick" book titles, all having subjective narratives regarding the subject.

In the past, I have read many similar books addressing financial education, sales, marketing, distribution, accounting, finance, etc. Still, I have always asked myself a question: is there a direct, straightforward recipe for success? Why do all these books not hitting it straight to the point?

In the book you are holding in your hands, there is a different approach. Browsing through its pages, you will find various ideas for creating businesses and the corresponding business plans for proper execution. With the aid of real examples that you can directly reproduce or modify, you will realize a successful business and generate revenues that you have never imaged before.

I promise, if you read this book thoroughly and followed up on the instructions that are disclosed within its pages, you will find yourself becoming an instant success.

You will start generating a new stream of income that may become your primary means of living. You may become an instant millionaire and help other people finding their way too.

"Less is more only when more is too much."
Frank Lloyd Wright

This book is short. I made it like that because I want you to read it cover to cover in a matter of hours. You may even reread it to reaffirm the useful ideas and strategies that could facilitate your immediate success.

"The best time to buy a fire extinguisher was yesterday."

We all should prepare ourselves to implement a new strategy to generate new income streams to secure our future and the future of our beloved ones before it is too late. Let this book be your companion for the upcoming few hours;

who knows, maybe it will spark new ideas that could change your life dramatically. Just give it a chance!

It will be my pleasure to receive your feedback, success stories, ideas, and concerns at any time. Drop me an email at [info@intellifields.com,](info@intellifields.com) and I will personally feed you back as soon as possible.

To your success;

Mohamed Kamar

INTRODUCTION

We live in the era of entrepreneurship. Smart and successful business owners prosper, while average employees struggle.

Naysayers will keep preaching the same old recipes of disaster: "Get super educated and join a multinational corporation." Climb the corporate ladder slowly, secure a steady stream of income, and secure a pension that will support you when you most need it.

"There are two types of people who will tell you that you cannot make a difference in this world: those who are afraid to try and those who are afraid you will succeed."
Ray Goforth

It became clear day after day that multinational corporations will keep downsizing employees due to advancements in technology (almost all production lines and deskwork are becoming automated by using software).

The outsourcing of cheap foreign workforce made high-wage employees a liability for employers. Governmental corporations are vanishing; job security is no longer the norm of the day compared to the good old days.

Sounds scary, right? Yes. Accurate? You bet. When you are betting your life and the lives of your beloved ones against the odds of a system that might fail at any time, you certainly have to worry. When you are betting your life and the lives of your beloved ones on a moody, abusive, and toxic manager, you certainly have to worry. When you are betting your life and the lives of your beloved ones on economic and political hurdles, you certainly have to worry.

This book is the distillation of a true-life experience, where I have had the opportunity to set myself free from the slavery of employment through smart but straightforward strategies, which are weirdly noticeable. Still, no one has ever dared to mention them publicly. Maybe it is the secret of all secrets to keep your tricks to yourself to amass more and more wealth.

I decided that it is the time to give it all back to the people who are the reason for my riches and success, knowing that giving is the best way to gain.

THE AMBITIOUS TEACHER

Almost fifteen (15) years back, immediately after receiving my Bachelor's degree in science (major in chemistry), I started my professional life. Like other people, I told myself, enough education, it is the time to make money.

Although I have always been fascinated with the science of chemistry and dreamed of being a chemist and inventing something that could contribute to people's happiness, I was obliged to take another route. I became a teacher!

I chose to be a teacher because there is always a market for chemistry teachers, especially those who can simplify the "complicated stuff." The rewards were fair, and the job was easy. I made a fast decision to join this career, although it was not my ambition to be a teacher by any means.

Full of motivation and inspiration, knowing that I can express my uniqueness (teaching is a one-man show, as the saying goes). I diligently and passionately started teaching chemistry in reputable multinational schools and began to earn some decent money. I loved my students, and my students loved me, and life was heaven.

Little did I know that I will struggle in the rigid systems of schools for five years, moving from one school to another in an attempt to find a different mentality that fosters innovation and creativity.

I remember Mrs. V, "my ex-supervisor," who happened to be a senior biology teacher; nevertheless, she supervises chemistry and physics teachers! When she insisted that teachers should read from the textbook during sessions. She said, "teachers are not allowed to propose any different teaching methodologies rather than that mentioned in the textbook."

Later on, I realized that she was doing so only to satisfy a teacher who was struggling to deliver chemistry properly to the other classes' students.

> "Any business today that embraces the status quo as an operating principle is going to be on a death march."
> Howard Schultz

I told her that we had attended many teaching methodology sessions from the accreditation organization that confirms that whenever teachers refer to the textbook in front of their students, they instantly lose their credibility. On the other hand, when teachers stand up tall and deliver, they radiate vibes of confidence and reliability.

Unfortunately, as you may have expected, Mrs. V told me you have to stick with the curriculum line by line. She said such accreditation procedures are only colorful stuff that the accreditation organization brainwashes people's minds with. It was the straw that broke the camel's back. I just felt that there is something rotten in the state of Denmark, and things won't work this way any longer.

I remember reading a book titled **"If you want to be rich and happy, don't go to school,"** by **Robert Kiyosaki,** which I have found weirdly cutting straight to the bones of my dilemma.

> "I owe my success to having listened respectfully to the very best advice, and then going away and doing the exact opposite."
> G. K. Chesterton

I just thought for a while, I have failed in something that I don't want to spend my life doing, instead of trying to seize my dreams and venture to the unknown land of entrepreneurship.

By the way, there is nothing wrong with obeying systems. However, it feels awful when you recognize a chance for improvement, and you propose it to your boss to be surprised by rejection because you are breaking the status quo.

"Here's to the crazy ones. The misfits. The rebels. The troublemakers. The round pegs in the square holes. The ones who see things differently. They're not fond of rules. And they have no respect for the status quo. You can quote them, disagree with them, glorify or vilify them. About the only thing you can't do is ignore them. Because they change things, they push the human race forward. And while some may see them as the crazy ones, we see genius. Because the people who are crazy enough to think they can change the world are the ones who do."

Rob Siltanen

The problem is that the previously mentioned structure was that of the industrial age termed as "Standard Operating Procedures," which apply only on industrial production lines. Those procedures are no more valid in the information age.

The information age that we are currently living in is far different from the industrial age. Later in this book, we will understand that this digital age eliminated the unfair advantage of the know-how and industrial secrets. Today, you can search for "How to make a homemade Coca Cola," and Google will give you 13,100,000 results (in 0.55 seconds).

Nowadays, employers know very well that you can manage to do all the necessary work remotely from your home, with a performance even better than showing up physically at the office.

Nothing will provide more evidence to the effectiveness of working remotely than what is happening right now with the worldwide outbreak of the COVID-19 pandemic that forced corporations to adopt remote working.

Again, I am not against the idea of employment, but I am against a system that is obsolete and has expired since a long time ago. Still, no one has the guts to question it, especially when you are the employee and report to an employer.

Furthermore, this old obsolete system is not cultivating talent. It also follows a standard that rewards employees that follow these rules without any deviations even if such variations are for the good of the business (not generalizing, but I am quite sure that my idea strikes you).

Since there are no innovation and breakthroughs, private multinational organizations realized the above mentioned and are now outsourcing low wage employees from other countries to do all the necessary office works remotely. The world is flat!

Moreover, the employment atmosphere is always competitive and not cooperative. You won't be able to convince me otherwise. Such atmospheres promote the literal zero-sum game where someone's success will lead to someone else's underrating. Only with few exceptions and good management practices, such conflict of interest could be managed on a minimal number of occasions.

Sounds brutal or unethical, right? Still, this is the brutal reality that everyone is trying to conceal.

Employers will always refer to those lovely words like teamwork and say that the company is looking for those individuals who can cooperate with their teammates to reach their goals.

> "Teamwork is the glue that binds losers together."
>
> Felix Dennis

From experience, many companies are just looking for the necessary work of a given employee. That's why they will always refer to those lovely expressions that hypnotize people until they reach their goal; whenever the work is done, the companies will downsize employees to minimize their overheads, definitely with few exceptions.

The problem is that we always think that we are exceptional and our companies are also unique. Unfortunately, the reality is far from this.

I just thought for a while again that starting a business promotes leadership, real teamwork, cooperation, innovation, and entrepreneurship. The same happens with the newly established companies where the number of players is limited, and every player knows his/her roles and responsibilities without any conflict of interest.

> **"The Only Thing That Is Constant Is Change ."**
> **Heraclitus**

That's why I resigned; I still remember my resignation wording line by line:

"I hereby notify you that I am sorrowfully resigning for personal reasons. It was an honor working at your schools."

Fortunately, the administrator tearfully didn't accept my resignation and gave me a lecture about the importance of my presence with the team and the students, giving me time to prepare! During this time, I read like never before all sorts of business books that I could lay my hands on to prepare for the next step. I knew very well that I am counting my days in this place.

When the time came, I left the school for once and forever and started my own business. I told myself it doesn't matter how small the venture is; as long as I am promoting something valuable to the people who trust me, I will always generate enough money to break even.

Additionally, small scale ventures act as a school for many aspects of understanding business; the most important of them is selling, which we will detail later on.

I started to read more about business, entrepreneurship, sales, marketing, simple accounting, finance, and incorporating companies until I started my second business venture, which luckily was an ultra-success. The venture has instantly shifted me literally from "zero to hero."

Suddenly, I became a superstar among my friends and family members; I was free to read, think, and choose.

"Readers are Leaders."

"Because to take away a man's freedom of choice, even his freedom to make the wrong choice, is to manipulate him as though he were a puppet and not a person."
Madeleine L'Engle

Choice is the best feeling in this whole world. You are no more trapped in this rat race day in and day out to meet ends. You are not obliged anymore to wake up early to go to work and sign in, stay those agonizing hours "sometimes without any reason," and sign out to fulfill those bureaucratic procedures required to keep employees ordered and disciplined following their employer's rules.

That's why I have made this book to open your imagination to the infinite possibilities of being a producer. Imagine giving salaries instead of receiving ones and being at the drivers' wheel instead of being driven.

Caution: this is not an invitation to quit your job right away; on the contrary, it is essential in the beginning to keep your day job and start a part-time business. First, you have to test the waters of your prototype; once your efforts pay off, you can rely solely on your business to build your empire slowly but surely.

Note: my book is not a formulations manuscript rather than a mind-opening vehicle for anyone who has adjusted his frequency to success and freedom. First, I recommend reading this book cover to cover; then, you can browse whatever part has stricken an idea in your mind and give it more attention and focus.

Additionally, it will be essential to read the recommended books listed at the end to receive the full integration of knowledge to boost your possibilities for quick success. Notwithstanding this, you should execute a project at the earliest convenience possible; otherwise, you will be a library of books walking down the street.

This book distills every piece of wisdom I could put my hands on to share a unique journey of success with you and help you enjoy the same kind of triumph and much more only if you gave yourself the chance to read and imagine the possibilities.

I hope this book will prove valuable wherever life takes you.

Mohamed Kamar

Dr. D. A

While I was a school teacher, I went to my local café only to meet an old high-school colleague. We greeted each other, and like all other conversations of the same nature, each of us asked the other about his progress in life. I told him that I am currently working as a high school chemistry teacher and concealed my misfortune.

To my surprise, he told me that he started his business by establishing a pharmaceutical factory. Wow! Since the subject was interesting to me, I didn't hesitate to ask him every kind of question. I asked him what kind of products he manufactures and how in the world could he get a license for such a manufacturing facility while he is still young? Because I know very well that pharmaceuticals are the most challenging manufacturing license to be granted.

He told me that he registered only two products, "Acetone, which is a nail polish remover" & "Glycerin, which is a skin moisturizer." He told me that he is on his way to registering other similar products.

I wondered and asked, are these two products capable of giving you the critical mass of cash flow that will make you meet ends and stay in business, covering overheads and all other expenses?

To my surprise, he told me that such simple products are being sold like commodities, and the same generate a substantial amount of revenue that covers all operating expenses and give him the chance to expand.

The conversation was highly exciting; I thanked him for his time. He left the cafe, but I stayed and kept thinking!

I wondered, although these products are being sold in bulk at chemical stores with very high purity and low price, the lack of knowledge of the customers made the hidden hand of the market to play its magic making fortunes to the knowledgeable only (an unfair advantage).

The only difference that Dr. D.A did is packaging these chemicals to appeal to the targeted customers he is pursuing. Is this real? Is that true?

In this sense, we will have this unfair advantage of knowledge to work in our favor by imitating others' success uniquely, making something new and novel.

Two parts divides this book:

Part I: will take you directly to the journey of building up your first venture out of the blue. This part will drive you to the market place as soon as possible. This part will require you to read the whole section to get a good background about the whole idea of repackaging.

Part II: embraces the required knowledge for any businessman to become successful. I refer to it periodically to remind myself of the knowledge and wisdom that guides me if I went astray.

Remember that starting a business doesn't require an idea only to move on. Still, it requires you to cultivate many other qualities progressively to gain a successful entrepreneur's attitude. This part is a distillation of many readings and life experiences related to those essential subjects. You can revisit this part anytime and browse its pages randomly, knowing that each page will benefit you one way or another.

Such wisdom distillates many authors' sweat, blood, and tears; just don't underestimate it.

"The only thing about a man that is a man . . . is his mind. Everything else you can find in a pig or a horse."
Archibald MacLeish

PART 1

WHY REPACKAGING?

Repackaging
Definition (Dictionary & Merriam Webster):

Noun
- The process of packaging goods again or differently.
"The repackaging of the juice brand was well-received."
- The presentation of a person or thing in a new way.
"Constant reworking and repackaging of ideas."

Verb
- Package again or differently.
"Excess stock may be given to charities or repackaged."
- Present in a new way.
"The commission has repackaged its ideas."

Transitive verb
- to package again or anew

Accurately: to put into a more efficient or attractive form

If you are busy doing something right now, I invite you to stop for a moment, clear up your mind and try to think of the definition and meaning of packaging and repackaging.

Life itself is all about something bounding other things. Starting from atoms up to the most sophisticated products, it is all about enclosures.

Do a simple, straightforward exercise now that will directly hit the idea to the point:

- Choose any product you can see in your bathroom, whether it be a toothpaste, a deodorant, shaving cream, hair oil, gel, antiseptic, detergent, or anything found there. Look at the back of the product; you will find the word "ingredients" or "contains," which enlist all the chemicals and products included in the composition.

- Pick up a medicine pamphlet and read the active ingredients of this medicine. You will find that the capsule or pill includes several substances that are considered the active ingredients that cure the illness. A mixture of active substances bound in an enclosure called a capsule. The capsule is the package. Sometimes such pills or capsules contain nothing (placebo); ironically, they cure illness psychologically!

- The tea you are drinking right now or the coffee cup in front of you contains an active substance, caffeine, responsible for its uplifting and nourishing properties. Professionally packaged and branded, tea and coffee both are the favorite hot beverages of the world.

- Look to the pen you are writing with now; it is an enclosure of a "stain" called ink, which is responsible for giving you the utility to register your thoughts on a piece of paper or a napkin* in order not to forget them later on.

* The best ideas have always been registered on such things.

Imagine now that you could outsource the above mentioned and put them in another package, sometimes with additional additives that make your product a standalone version out of competition (e.g., tea + flavors) brand the same with a unique registered name of yours. Does this have the potential to be a success?

How about knowing that one substance can make a ridiculous number of products that could be packaged, branded, and marketed for success.

For example, Ethyl Alcohol or Beer Alcohol, "known as Ethanol," can be used in a ridiculous number of products:
- 1- Alcoholic beverages;
- 2- Detergent;
- 3- Mouth Wash;
- 4- Antiseptic;
- 5- Coolant;
- 6- Antifreeze;
- 7- Thermometer material for measuring low temperatures;
- 8- Goo gone ingredient;
- 9- Perfume;
- 10- Fuel by itself or as an ingredient of energy;
- 11- Solvent for many chemicals;
- 12- Screen cleaner;
- 13- Dehydrating agent;
- 14- Hand Sanitizer;
- 15- Anesthetic...etc.

The list can go on and on. You can enumerate countless uses for a single substance, which means numerous products based on the same material.

We will talk about generating countless uses out of one single substance using the ultimate tool, mind mapping later.

In that sense, we will start Part I of this book by exploring how we would start a business "whether it be large or small" based on this simple universal understanding.

I have selected physical products as an example of starting a business, but the idea of repackaging is not only restricted to physical products. You know the names of many software products and know too their alternatives. Developers have also followed the same "Secret" of repackaging, and many of them are now reaping its fruits. For instance, Mark Zuckerberg repackaged Hi5 to Facebook, Brian Acton and Jan Koum (former employees of Yahoo) repackaged BlackBerry Messenger to WhatsApp, and the list goes on.

If you are one of those developers, trust me, you can apply repackaging to your software too. I am not promoting plagiarism; on the contrary, I am promoting creativity and novelty. Many software we are using daily lack many essential features; we just say to ourselves if only this or that feature was included, it will make a big difference.

One day, I sent to the largest instant messaging mobile application company an email recommending to include an automatic reply feature (for example: in a meeting, sleeping, busy, will call you back later) and not just a status that could facilitate communication with other people. Up till now, the developers didn't include such an essential feature.

Maybe you can develop such software that will be very important for business owners and employees, and such software will find the interest of those professional people. You can become the next software guru.

The good news is that we are in the information age and that all the required information is at our disposal. We used to say that software development is only for those who were fortunate to study programming at college or those nerd people who have inherited their parents' careers.

To our amusement now, we always hear about self-taught programmers who have developed world-class software that profoundly impacted our lives. Thanks to simple programming languages like **Python** and **R** where their codes resemble the English language. You can now download a Bootcamp course for Python, think of a project, and start working on it after only one week of studying the language's syntax and its fundamentals.

> **"Simplicity is the soul of efficiency."**
> **Austin Freeman**

I know that you may have some doubts about studying in just a few weeks and the capability to develop a full operating software that provides great utility to its users. Right?

I used to have the same doubts; until I have developed my first software using Python, I have developed a powerful email extractor. The software can extract email addresses from different file formats and any URL. I won't tell you how powerful the software is, and I am sure it will fascinate anyone using it. You will be able to download it shortly from my website (www.intellifields.com).

I have developed software after only two months of studying Python. I have practiced Python coding almost two hours per day, and the trick is to start immediately with a meaningful project. You don't have to keep coding calculators or Hello world kind of stuff.

By the way, I have also developed my website using the same languages mentioned above, but the process was much easier indeed.

Even book authors repackage! I know a well-known author who wrote a best selling book and made almost twenty other books with different titles, including the same information in the first book with only slight modifications here and there. He simply repackaged his words.

I bet you heard about this book titled **"Everything men know about women" by Dr. Alan Francis** has 128 completely blank pages. Published in 1989, the book claims to "reveal the most comprehensive understanding of men's knowledge and understanding of the opposite sex." The book has a rating of 4.3 out of 5 on Amazon's book discovery platform Goodreads. Can you believe this? The "author" repackaged blank papers and gave them a title and became a millionaire because of that.

Notwithstanding all of the above, I have succeeded dramatically in the physical products arena as it is not rocket science. I believe it is far easier and needs no unique talents to execute compared to coding and writing.

Again, don't think the above mentioned is a copycat game scheme; on the contrary, the products you will create are the free market's essence. The same is for all customers and buyers' welfare, as we will see later on in this book.

So, enough introductions, and let us dive straight to the invention of our first saleable product.

TYPE OF GOODS

Before venturing through, we have to understand key concepts about the trade of physical goods locally and internationally.

There are two significant groups of physical goods:

COMMODITIES (NEEDS)

They are the "essentials," which are traded on a bulk basis exclusively between governments and large traders who have the financial ability to execute such deals.

For example, Food (grains, vegetable oil, sugar, vegetables, fruits, and the like), Petrochemicals, Fertilizers, Feed, Fuel, Construction Material, Metals, Minerals, and many others are listed on the stock exchanges with well-known market prices.

Since commodities have well-known published prices, large traders know that trading such goods is much toward investing (cash on cash returns) rather than inventing an entrepreneurial business (entrepreneurial ventures require smartness and wit to create value out of nothing). Since the margins are meager, the profits are only realized by handling bulk quantities (hundreds of thousands of tons), restricting startups from approaching such markets.

Although trading commodities require no brains, the competition in this arena is very stiff, "The literal Zero-Sum Game."

> "Commodities such as gold and silver have a world market that transcends national borders, politics, religions, and race. A person may not like someone else's religion, but he'll accept his gold."
> Robert Kiyosaki

NICHE (WANTS)

They are the products that fall in the category of non-essentials, for example, expensive perfumes, cosmetics, nutritional supplements, accessories, a particular brand of coffee, a unique brand of food, and almost all kinds of products that play on the emotions of the people rather than their real needs.

Additionally, niche market customers never think of price as a primary factor for their buying decision. Hence, you will always see millions of people using the latest iPhones, driving Porshe, wearing Rolex.

To your surprise, we are drowning in a giant sea of niche products. Look around you right now and do a simple exercise: write down a list of niche products surrounding you and trust me when I say your paper won't hold the whole list.

For me, my solution to this exercise just right now is as follows:

- Branded mp3 player,
- Branded Cellphone,
- Branded perfume,
- Branded Desktop PC,
- Branded Laptop,
- Branded coffee,
- Branded corrector pen,
- Branded cleaning wipes,
- Branded green tea,
- Branded white shirt,
- Branded shoes,
- Branded power bank for cellphones,
- Branded watch,

- Branded wallet,
- Branded chocolate bar,
- And even Branded pain killers.

Although essentials are vital in our lives but non-essentials dominate!

Knowledgeable Businessmen realized this fact about the insanity of human thinking and decided to work on it to amount fortunes for themselves and for future generations to come.

Note: there is nothing unethical in knowing that people think in such a manner. You think the same way. To prove this, ask yourself now which brand of fragrance you most likely prefer to wear if you attend an important event? If you answered this question, then, "Welcome to the Club."

It is ethical to understand human nature and use this insider knowledge; many people will keep telling you it is unfair to sell people useless things to gain fortunes. To cut things short for such losers, never listen to those people, they will only waste your time and energy, and once they are in financial stress, they will look for a friend like you to lend them money!

Additionally, you won't sell or promote useless stuff. Together we will make useful products that add value to our customers, and the good news is that these products will be much cheaper than the existing ones.

Turning Dust to Gold

The ultimate business of all times is always related to the conversion of a commodity to a niche. The like of turning dust to Gold.

For example:

1. Urea is a well-known commodity fertilizer used to provide Nitrogen to the soil. Its price is fixed (today's average price is $260/ton) as a fertilizer.

   Fortunately, Urea can be used to manufacture multiple niche products. Instant cold packs (first aid item to treat burns and Bruises) magnifies its profit margin at least 200X. All that you have to do is to put loose urea granules and a closed water pack inside the same package; upon puncturing the internal water pack, water mixes with Urea starting the freezing effect (an endothermic reaction).

   The same goes for Ammonium Nitrate, but this chemical's trade is hazardous as it is a precursor of many types of explosives. I would instead use Urea in my product to avoid any hassles in the registration of the product.

   Note: to further reduce the price of manufacturing Instant cold packs; some manufacturers use off-spec Urea. Suppliers will be pleased to sell you such an off-spec product and will never think that you are multiplying the value of such a rejected product by hundreds of times.

   As the saying goes: **"one man's trash is another man's treasure."** You can search for factories nearby you and ask for their byproducts. A whole new industry could be created from such valuable byproducts.

2. Calcium Chloride (a byproduct of the Soda Ash industry) is another commodity chemical with a low market price used mainly as a deicing salt in European Countries.

   Fortunately, Calcium Chloride can be used to manufacture Instant hot packs the same way as Urea.

   Hot packs are used as a first-aid item that soothes muscle aches in case of muscle spasms.

3. Sand could be mixed with bentonite clay (which is another commodity) and packaged in beautiful looking bags, and sold as cat litter.

4. Barium Sulfide, another common chemical, is the main ingredient of hair depilatory and shaving creams. The problem is that it smells like rotten eggs. If you can add something to mask such smell, the world will pay you in compensation.

5. Peppermint oil is sold in bulk to toothpaste and candies factories, but it could be repackaged in 10 ml bottles as a breath freshener that could multiply its value hundreds of times. Similarly, eugenol (the essential oil of clove) can be used in this regard as another flavor.

6. Boric Acid is a well-known chemical that is used as a fertilizer. Mixing boric acid with a dough of flour, powdered milk, sugar make the ultimate cockroach and ants bait you could ever imagine. You can do some modifications with the ingredients of the dough using mashed chicken liver (cockroaches adore it)

7. Acetone is an excellent organic solvent. With color and odor additives, it becomes a nail polish remover sold in 10 ml bottles hundreds of times more expensive than its original price as a raw material.

8. Toluene, another organic solvent, can be easily mixed with gasoline and sold as an Octane booster.

9. Hydrogen Peroxide is a powerful antiseptic used to disinfect wounds. Although dentists recommend its usage by patients occasionally, a limited number of mouth wash products include this active substance are available in the market. With few additives like color and flavors suitable with hydrogen peroxide, a new product could be used extensively by this broad market.

* Note: for any formulations intended for human consumption, you should be careful with the amounts of ingredients you are using. Such measurements are a prerequisite for registering the product, as we will see a few pages ahead.

An excellent tip I always use while manufacturing products for human consumption, I simply ask myself, will I be able to use this product myself and to let my parents and beloved ones use it too? If the answer is yes, I immediately start working confidently on the project; if not, I have to reconsider everything.

"To invent, you need a good imagination and a pile of junk."
Thomas A. Edison

Repackaging the products mentioned above and thousands of others into new products and selling them to local and export markets could generate millions of dollars in revenue only to those who have the guts to apply the repackaging strategy.

You may be wondering how I could know the uses of chemicals to follow the above mentioned rational? The answer is simple; you can download a condensed chemical dictionary or The Merck Index and always search for uses.

Now, if you are convinced with the idea of repackaging and want to start your own business, I can assure you that you have made the right decision reading this book because I will assist you now in the most straightforward way ever on how to make your dreams come true.

BLOCK FLOW DIAGRAM

Before venturing through, I invite you to review the Block Flow Diagram below, which summarizes the book's next parts. You will understand that many activities need to be done before starting any actual works. We will term these activities as the Pre-execution works. The pre-execution works will end by selecting a product that has a very high potential for success.

After the product selection, you will enter the Project phase to transform the idea into a real physical product.

Once you have the product, you will start marketing and selling it to the potential buyers in the operation phase.

Let's explore each phase individually to know all the required activities and their impact on the repackaging venture.

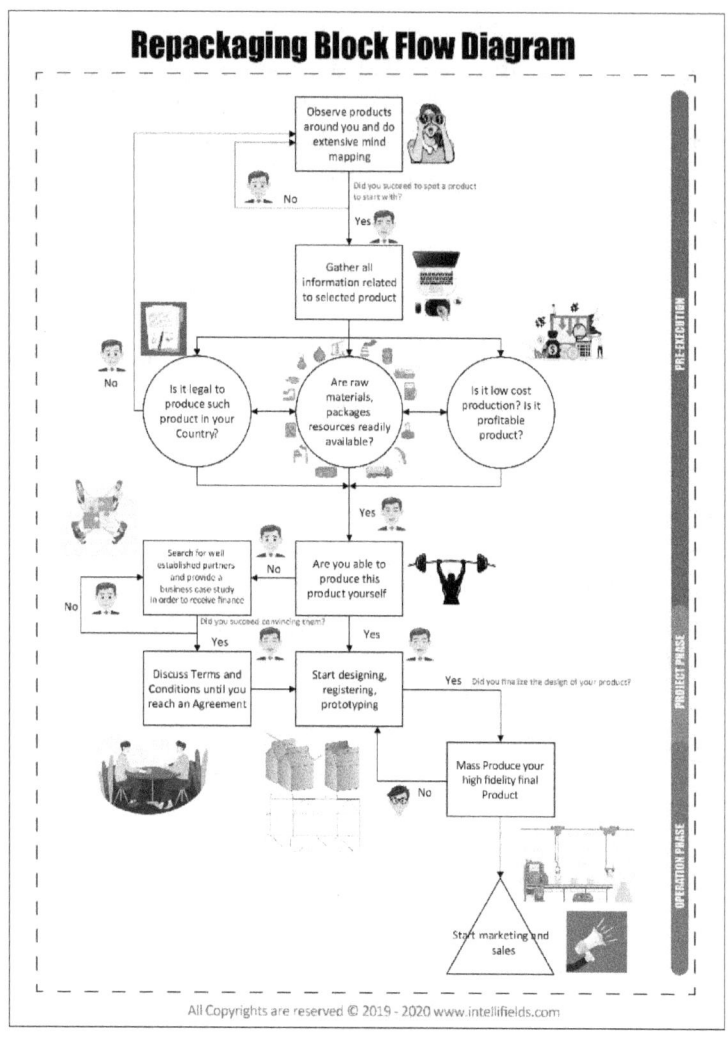

PRE-EXECUTION WORKS
SELECTING YOUR PRODUCT

Well, many readers will think that this is the hardest part of the development. Trust me when I tell you, on the contrary, that this is the easiest part.

Why is it the easiest part? Because we are following the idea of repackaging. Products already exist in front of you, and you have the freedom of choice to select the ones that you think having strong potential for success and pursue them. While I am sipping my coffee cup now, I am doing the same exercise you will be doing in selecting your potential products, and I can assure you that the choices are plenty beyond your imagination.

I invite you to bring a blank paper and write down all the products that surround you right now. Stop writing when you reach twenty (20) items, at least. Ask yourself, is there one item of the twenty listed has the potential to be your next repackaged product? After doing so, ask yourself, what can I do to improve this current product?

For example, I can see a brown shoe polish cream that could be a potential repackaging project. I can add fragrance to its components to make the shoe gleam and release agreeable adore. I can also add a wiping cloth with the package instead of the sponge only.

On the other hand, you can follow the previously mentioned execution plan to make a brand new product. The keyword here is idea generation.

Ideas come and go every day, and they are not restricted to the so-called geniuses. The difference which makes the great difference is to think of generating ideas intentionally.

Ask yourself, do I make it a habit to bring a blank paper or a piece of napkin and write my ideas on them to keep a repository of ideas for future implementation if possible? Did I pen at the top of a paper a problem and thought about the different ways to solve it? If you did, you are already on your way to succeed, but if you didn't, you should make it a habit to register whatever thoughts or ideas that could come to your mind. It doesn't matter how absurd the ideas are; just don't limit yourself.

> **"We first make our habits, and then our habits make us."**
> **John Dryden**

One day, I worked as a member of the project management team to develop a billion dollars industrial project sponsored by the government, and an unavoidable technical problem has happened. All team members thought of the dramatic negative impact the problem will cause on the facilities' operations and the respective financial losses.

I told a senior manager, **"there are a hundred ways to kill the cat."** I went to my favorite local café and ordered my usual double espresso. On the small squared piece of napkin that has come with the coffee, I wrote the problem. Then listed the reasons for its cause (they term it root cause analysis) and won't tell you that the well-known quote **"a problem well stated is a problem half solved"** has played its magic. I spotted the real reason for the problem immediately and started to think of workarounds until I reached an ultimate solution. I won't tell you how much joy and happiness I experienced while I was halfway sipping my coffee. I immediately called the project manager and told him that I would propose a solution tomorrow at the office.

The next day, the proposal has been scrutinized by the whole technical teams and the project manager. Almost 90% doubted its implementation, and only 10% said it might work.

I traveled the next week to the United States to discuss the proposed solution with the technology providers. To my surprise and the surprise of everyone, the proposed solution worked out. The same resolution was also recommended by a leading Belgian Company working on the same project, which further satisfied my ego.

> "First they ignore you, then they laugh at you, then they fight you, then you win."
> Mahatma Gandhi

Ideas are free; they are crawling right now around our heads. You just have to adjust your frequency to receive them and, more importantly, register them in order not to lose them.

> "Everything Begins With An Idea."
> Earl Nightengale

For our journey, I am proposing two subtle means of thinking to generate ultimate ideas and products:

Top-Down thinking
In Top-Down thinking, you start your thinking with the final marketable product. Then you exert your full efforts to know all the raw materials required, preparation methods, and proper packaging.

Bottom-Up thinking
In Bottom-Up thinking, you start thinking with the ingredients (raw materials and necessary chemicals) that you can outsource locally with a minimum cost. Then you further think of all potential products that could be derived from it.

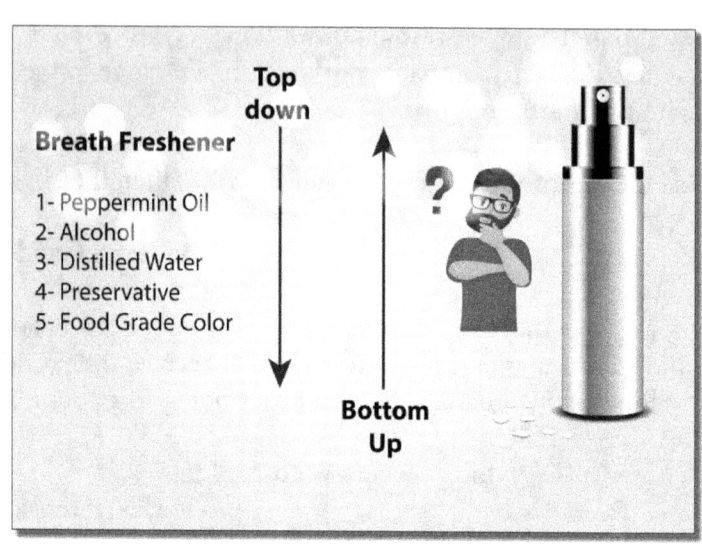

Breath Freshener

1- Peppermint Oil
2- Alcohol
3- Distilled Water
4- Preservative
5- Food Grade Color

Top down

Bottom Up

MIND MAPPING FOR SUCCESS

I didn't realize how powerful this brainstorming technique is for the creation of new ideas.

The idea is to put a central Keyword and start creating branches of thoughts out of it, and each branch creates further sub-branches until all your thoughts are compiled in one wonderfully demonstrated page.

Here is an example of a typical mind mapping way of thinking I have done once to generate niche products:

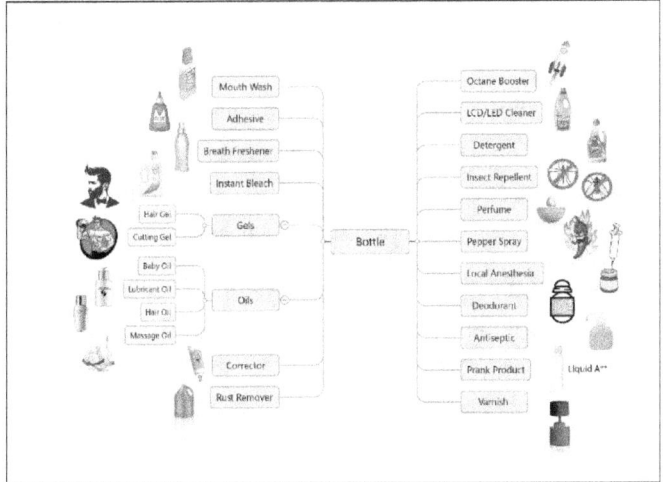

(This is an example of the top-down way of thinking)

Did you get the idea? To your knowledge, while drafting this mind map right now, I got a new niche product idea that I believe will make me fortunes **(But I cannot tell you, or I will have to kill you).**

Did you see it? I said, "I believe" because to say that the idea is feasible, you have to follow the previously mentioned Block Flow Diagram to assess the feasibility.

I won't tell you about summarizing whole books after reading them into mind maps.

Note: you don't have to buy any special software or a bunch of colored pens to mind map; you can start drawing your plans on a napkin at your local café; maybe such a piece of tissue will include the fortunes that you have always dreamed about.

> "Imagination is more important than knowledge. Knowledge is limited. Imagination encircles the world."
> Albert Einstein

They say that: **"Necessity is the mother of invention; I would rather say insanity is the mother of invention."** Don't delimit yourself; imagine and let your mind soar with new ideas. Just remember to write them down and save them.

The more subtle ideas pop up in your mind, the more the chances you will end up with a superstar business that will pay off in the future.

	Two Brains that you have

You have to distinguish between two brains: your creative brain and the other is the editing brain.

The creative brain is responsible for the generation of ideas. It doesn't care about polishing them to appeal to the audience. This brain is concerned with the creation of new ideas or the improvement of the existing ones.

Hence, while generating ideas, don't ever think of editing,

polishing, spell checking, reviewing grammar, designing, and coloring. Just focus on the most crucial task, which is creating more smart ideas.

On the other hand, the Editing Brain; it is the part of your brain, which is concerned with polishing everything. This one doesn't think creatively; instead, it reasons professionally. If you have designed a rough prototype, this brain starts to refine such design with more narratives, more drawings, more adjustments to the fonts, grammar, and the like.

While you are thinking of new ideas, try to keep the editing brain idle as much as possible to let the other creative mind fly high to the skies of inspiration.

I have implemented the same kind of strategy while I am writing this book. First, you have to make a rough draft of your chapters; then, you must polish them.

"To err is human; to edit, divine."

	Focus

When you start your efforts thinking for new ideas to generate new products or optimize existing ones, you must exercise deep thinking. Deep thinking is defined in many books, which is sometimes referred to as slow thinking. That type of thinking requires you to pay the most attention and exert some super mental efforts to conclude something tangible.

Such deep thinking requires some essential conditions that should be highlighted to get the most out of your efforts.

First, you have to clear your mind from anything other than the exercise at hand. Typically, the human mind cannot think of two things simultaneously.

The second and most important thing is that you have to avoid distractors as a plague. Nothing is worse than you being genuinely thinking while suddenly something pops up to distract you.

Thinking is like drilling a hole on earth mining for diamonds. You could be mining in the right place at the right time until a distractor pops up, and all your efforts are futile. You could be calculating the critical mass of the atomic bomb when all of a sudden, you receive an instant message on your cellphone, your email client notifies you with a new email, or your wife shouts, asking you to pick up the garbage.

Sure, you have experienced one time in your life the computer progress bar's progressing until it reaches 99% when something goes wrong, and you have to start downloading or installing the software again.

I would highly recommend it when you decide to exercise deep thinking to find a proper place. Your home, office, or even a local café, are perfect. Still, it would help if you told people around you that you are doing a critical exercise or a piece of work that requires no distraction at all except for a dire emergency.

Switch off your mobile (or turn on don't disturb mode, which allows few exceptions). Make yourself a cup of coffee or hot tea. Support yourself with all tools like pens, pencils, notes, rubber. And don't let anyone disturb you, for God's sake.

In a few cases, when it is impossible to control other people's sound (i.e., in a café or while kids are playing at home), you could easily use earplugs or turn on some "white noise" in the background to overshadow the nasty sounds of distractors. Some examples of white noise are thunderstorms; rain sounds with ocean waves, campfire. My favorite is Fan noise.

> The only prudence in life is concentration."
> Emerson

THINK OF COMPLEMENTARY PRODUCTS

When we always talk about new products and new ideas, people will always think of novel things. Of course, novel products and services will have great potential for success if the subject novel idea reached a target market that could understand such an idea's novelty. For example, the iPod was one of a kind product that introduced the concept of an online music store.

But let's talk about an easier way to generate substantial ideas and add considerable value to your customers. Complementary products complement the utility of a particular product and make use of the main product's existing market. For example, there are many screen cleaners (LED cleaners) with different colors and odors. Still, some cleaners have some additional complementary products that make cleaning far more manageable for the consumer to experience. A wiping textile and a brush are all that you have to add to be successful.

Painters prefer one brand of paint over a multitude of different reputable others. One day I asked the painter why all painters prefer this subject brand specifically; he smiled and said that the package design is broad, allowing painters to put all their tools inside it after it is empty.

While I am typing right now in the above few paragraphs, I eyed my keyboard. I remembered the thin plastic film covering the keyboard without compromising typing and how it could protect the keyboard from dirt and damage if any spill falls on it—an excellent example of a complementary product. You don't have to be Michael Dell or Steve Jobs to market your invention in the largest IT stores.

It may sound absurd, but give yourself the chance to think of the ideas mentioned above, and trust me, you could generate right now dozens of new complementary ideas that could make you an instant millionaire.

IDEAS' GENERATION ETHICS

It is worth mentioning that you have to think of beneficial products or services that will add real value to your customers if you are willing to succeed. I know many people who focus primarily on profits without focusing on adding any value to their customers. What those people do is a very short term venture that ruins their reputation. Deceive the customers who trusted you now, and I assure you that you will not return to the market again. Your good reputation is everything.

I am always puzzled with the internet scam artists who think of innovative ideas to scam their victims instead of using their intelligence to make something useful. Remember, it takes the same amount of time and effort to think of useful stuff rather than deceiving others.

I believe this is one of the critical elements of the success of the wealthiest people who have walked the earth. Those people thought of how they could improve other people's lives rather than making money. For them, money is only the byproduct of their contribution to the welfare of people.

See the example of Bill Gates, Steve Jobs, Sergey Brin, and Larry Page, Henry Ford. They were all shooting for a higher purpose, to provide a product or a service that authentically improve people's lives.

> **"The glue that holds all relationships together, including the relationship between the leader and the led, is trust, and trust is based on integrity."**
>
> Brian Tracy

IDEAS ALONE

It is said, **"A picture is worth a thousand words."** Please look carefully at the picture below and understand its meaning:

The problem is that the average person thinks that the reason for some people's success is their good ideas alone. They do not know that a good idea may be the least reason for their success. There are a lot of hidden activities that have to be done to succeed. Ideas in that sense are considered to be the tip of the iceberg. Titanic crew saw only the iceberg's spike and didn't consider what lies beneath, and they paid a high price.

No one can deny that a great idea could increase your chances of success. Still, it has to be executed and not only executed but also executed efficiently; otherwise, such great ideas will be kept hidden in the minds of their owners and will be buried with them the day they die.

> "Maybe you don't go to hell for the things you do. Maybe you go to hell for the things you don't do. The things you don't finish."
>
> Chuck Palahniuk

Hence, I would recommend it if you could read a little more about something called "Business Plan" or "Feasibility Study" to understand what I mean in the above mentioned few lines.

In a nutshell, a business plan is a document that addresses many aspects of a subject project, not only how appealing the idea of the project is. It addresses the following points:

1- The new venture location;
2- Cost of facilities (CAPEX) if any;
3- Cost of production (OPEX);
4- Permits and Licenses required;
5- Market study;
6- Profitability analysis (ROI, NPV, IRR, Payback period);

Business plans usually have a size ranging from few pages to thousands of pages depending on the project scale. Still, it is essential to dedicate the time to take a piece of paper and a pen and start writing down the table of contents of your business plan.

You will recognize that you didn't consider many things when you first thought of the idea. You could find opportunities and identify some risks. You can brainstorm to find workarounds or risk responses to mitigate such risks. You can even totally ignore the idea after discovering that you have missed an essential piece of information. In that sense, you can save your time, money, and efforts instead of climbing the wrong mountain.

That's why it is of primary importance not to skip such a step. I can assure you that later on in your life, you will write maybe dozens or even hundreds of these business plans for your ventures and the ventures of others "definitely, not for free."

> "Time is more valuable than money. You can get more money, but you cannot get more time".
>
> Jim Rohn

	Mr. H. R.

I have a friend of mine running a ladies clothes business that has been struggling for years. He was talented in writing business plans. He told me one day that he kept writing business plans for every idea until he became an expert writing such document with the associated financial models (which is a Microsoft Excel sheet, by the way).

I met him by accident after three years, and to my surprise, he told me that he runs a multimillion international business writing business plans for others. He told me he has almost 30 employees, and most of his clients are coming from the internet.

He told me that some governments assigned him to conduct audits on business plans and financial models as an independent consultant to provide his expert judgment.

You can assign others to write your business plan for you. Still, I would recommend writing at least the table of content of such a document.

Additionally, as I have mentioned before, business plans and project documents could easily help you find a strategic investor, partner, or financial institution. Those people are looking for something to read and will not accept a verbal explanation.

Apart from the importance of learning the anatomy of such a useful document, you have to keep your business idea on a low profile, especially if it has simple secrets that could be imitated easily.

Trust me when I tell you that your business idea could be easily stolen if revealed to someone claiming to be an advisor. Unfortunately, I learned this the hard way. (lesson learned).

"There are two rules for success:
1. Never reveal everything you know."

CLASSIFYING PRODUCTS

Did you recognize from the previous mind map that almost all physical products being traded are made up of:

- Major portion made only of one (1) chemical that is readily available to buy as raw material from chemical stores; we will term these products "Straight," for example:

"Soap base, Detergents base, Perfumes (I mean the oil), Insecticides base, Air fresheners base, Food additives base, Salts and Minerals, and natural extracts...etc.

- Large portion made of two (2) or more basic chemicals, we will term these products "Blends." When the above mentioned basic chemicals combine, miracles could happen, for example:

    Detergent + Perfume = countless number of well-known branded detergents;

    Sand + Bentonite clay = countless number of well-known cat litter;

    Food + Preservative + Borax = the ultimate insect bait;

    Food + Preservative + Zinc Phosphide = Rat Last Meal "as one of my friends registered it" or a rodenticide.

We all know a well-known company that made billions of Dollars worldwide only by mixing three (3) things in a new package: Coffee + powdered milk + Sugar.

- And small portion made of specialty chemicals with sophisticated processes to manufacture under certain conditions like medicinal formulations, we will term them "sophisticated."

Honestly, I would instead start with "Straights" and "Blends" to reduce the hassle of raising capital, granting licenses, and exploring know-how and trade secrets.

Unless you are a savvy negotiator and you have a real unique, sophisticated product, then you can exert more efforts drafting a professional product description and a high-level business plan to approach potential investors, financiers, or manufacturers.

GATHER INFORMATION
Mind Mapping Again

The first step in the process was to select a high-level product that you are interested in making. Now you have to gather all information about it. Just google the hell out of it and demonstrate all such data in a mind map.

That is the democratizing of the means of production, as termed in the Book **"The Long Tail" by Chris Anderson.**

We live in the information age, and all know-how is publicly published through the internet. You are one click away from everything.

In the past (The industrial age), the problem that faced many startups is the lack of knowledge and know-how. The problem in those days (Information age) is not the lack of knowledge but its surplus. If you google something, you will find a lot of information more than you expected. Let us see now; try and type the word "local Anesthetic" in Google's search bar and see what I mean.

Hence, you have to exert some effort to scrutinize information, select the useful ones, and discard the noise.

Noise here means any side tempting information that could distract you from your target.

So the question now is: what are you waiting for? Just move on, start thinking of your product and google it and see how much information you will receive from this miraculous window at your disposal. Why won't you start reacting? Why won't you seize the opportunity to create your niche product now?

 **Google Patents**

Google Patents indexes more than 87 million patents and patent applications with full text from 17 patent offices.

These documents include the entire collection of granted patents and published patent applications from each database (which belong to the public domain). US patent documents date back to 1790, EPO and WIPO to 1978. Optical character recognition (OCR) has been performed on the older US patents to make them searchable. Google Translate has been used on all non-English patents to make the English translations searchable.

Google Patents also indexes documents from Google Scholar and Google Books and has machine-classified them with Cooperative Patent Classification codes for searching.

Simply, You can search expired patents, which include thousands of registered recipes for each and everything.

I made a cockroach bait using one of these expired patents and marketed the product locally as "Roachbuster."

The eternal question may be popping up in your mind now, what product should I start with?

The answer to this question lies inside your head; it is your call, whether you want to manufacture perfumes, detergent, soap, insecticides, ink, coffee, gadgets, widgets, chemicals.

No one would be able to provide you with his unique way of thinking unless you partnered with him. For partnership, see **BUSINESS STRATEGIES AND SHORTCUTS** to make the right decision regarding this life long relationship.

Another effective means to gather information is to buy it (if your product requires so). Some data are not for free still; You can consider such information as an asset.

Trust me when I tell you that if you combed the internet, but you couldn't find the required information on your niche product, it is worth buying such information because it will be harder for anyone to imitate. Additionally, such purchased know-how could provide you with ideas and insights about tons of other feasible products that could blow up your mind.

I remember I searched for information regarding perfume fixatives (additives that make the perfume last longer). Such a search led me to manufacture an exceptional product that made me fortunes literally.

ASSESS YOUR CAPABILITIES
LEGAL

As demonstrated in the execution Block Flow Diagram, you have to assess manufacturing's legal aspects in a given country before venturing through a selected potential product.

For example, you could easily manufacture pepper spray, but some governments consider it an illegal product and restrict its manufacturing and usage by ordinary citizens. Another example is fireworks; some governments completely bans its manufacturing altogether.

I recommend starting with a benign product that can be quickly registered without any hassle to boost your faith in the overall strategy and provide you with the financial means to begin more significant ventures later on.

AVAILABILITY

Start your business with raw materials readily available in your market. Trust me; you don't have to import chemicals to prototype to test your market. Use the readily available local resources: raw material, chemicals, packages, and printing houses. Never think of importing until you are 100% sure that it is worth it.

> "Measure twice, cut once."

FINANCE
Raising Capital for your venture

Many people won't take any step to pursue their dreams because of the issue of startup capital. You have to know that this will not be an issue for you because all the money needed at this stage is for prototyping and not to finance the whole venture. During prototyping, you have to spend the minimum amount of money. Some people spend $100 or a maximum of $200 to prototype. Always remember, you are creating something out of nothing.

I don't recommend any borrowing at this stage of development.

"Those who go a borrowing go a sorrowing."

Suppose you don't have the money, just labor and save it. Saving reminds me of the first rule in the book **"The Richest Man in Babylon,"** which states, "one-tenth of what you earn is yours to keep."

Additionally, it will be an excellent chance to train yourself to save money, a quality that all successful entrepreneurs have in common.

As we will see later in this book, driving luxurious cars and spending on useless stuff won't make you look rich. Only fools will be impressed with this kind of thing.

"Do not save what is left after spending; instead, spend what is left after saving."
Warren Buffett

Imagine that you have exerted a lot of effort writing an article that took you hours only to realize that you have switched off your PC without saving the document. That's the analogy of working hard then spending all the money generated from it on useless stuff.

I recommend you read the book **"Ready, Fire, Aim"** by **Michael Masterson** for frugality.

EXECUTION PLAN

As a startup, you have to know that there are two phases of any business venture:

PROJECT PHASE

It is the phase in which efforts are made to transform your idea into a sellable product with a market. This phase includes some essential steps that must be followed to ensure the success of the endeavor.

OPERATIONS PHASE

I would instead name this phase the selling phase because, as we will see afterward, selling is the most crucial aspect of running any business.

Notwithstanding this, it also includes additional activities that ensure your business idea's efficiency and smooth success.

PROJECT PHASE

To succeed in making your product and ensure beforehand such success, you have to follow a particular sequence in your execution plan to reach your ultimate goal. I have developed a straightforward but powerful method here, which constitutes the universal approach of Project execution following the PMI standards (Project Management Institute).

Do not panic; I will not teach you here rocket science or project management. The same will be just a smattering about how things work and how you can ensure a significant probability of success to yourself or your partners (if any).

To complete any project, you have to follow this chronological sequence of events:

Initiation - planning - execution - monitoring and controlling - closing.

Five main activities that most of us follow unconsciously to manage our daily micro-projects.

When you are at the office (suppose you are still an employee), and your boss asks you to update a document, for instance. You automatically and subconsciously put the above sequence of events to update the report.

You may ask your boss, why are we updating this document at this time? What are the main goals behind this? Are there any additional requirements that need to be done in the new revision to satisfy further specific goals in mind?

What is the overall benefit of such an update? To whom will this document be shared? And on and on. The same is simply called initiation.

INITIATION
Initiation is the process where you ask those many questions mentioned above and put high-level answers to every one of them to know the rationale behind doing something. You don't have to put the same in writing, but you have to ask yourself why I would start such a project, and you should have a clear answer to every question.

PLANNING
"Failing to plan is planning to fail."

It is not rocket science to make a plan and to follow it. Can you imagine yourself riding your car in the morning aimlessly and thinking that you will reach a definite destination at the end of the day? I do not think so.

Early in the morning, while you are eating your breakfast before you even think of driving your car, you plan your day. You ask yourself what activities should I do today to get the most out of my time. Then unconsciously, you prioritize such activities. You use common sense ordering the actions to reach the desired results you have planned for, and that is planning.

Planning is preparing beforehand what needs to be done? When is it to be done? How is it to be done? And who is going to do what?

Therefore, planning is not restricted to defining the activities you will execute "something called Scope." But it has everything to do with forecasting the duration of execution for every activity, "Scheduling." And to estimate the cost of each of the defined actions "Budgeting."

Additionally, in this development phase, you can determine the workforce "Resources" that will be doing such activities. Understand that you are not obliged to bring a whole team to execute your project.

I am reiterating that all of the Project Management activities can be done by yourself alone and in a timeframe that you won't even imagine. You don't have to write the same down, but you have to have an execution plan. The more detailed your project plan, the less likely you will fall into a mistake, **"common sense has to be exercised."**

> **"Planning is bringing the future into the present so that you can do something about it now."**
>
> Alan Lakein, author

EXECUTION

> **"A good plan, violently executed now, is better than a perfect plan tomorrow."**

George Patton

Execution is the phase where the clock starts ticking. You have planned your project very well, bringing all resources, designed everything to their final revision (called Rev. 0, by the way), and you are ready to start the actual work.

You may be surprised that this is the most straightforward phase of your project, only if you have thoroughly planned everything. You know everything that should be done at a specific time and with a particular sequence and even expect what would happen if things did not work out the way you planned (Risk Management). I remember well-planned projects that took less than 48 hours to be executed and provided me with substantial monetary outcomes.

The real tip here is to start execution aggressively. You may be surprised that many so-called entrepreneurs stop at the planning stage and never execute their successful plans. If you did an authentic job planning, you should not be afraid to implement.

> **"Leaders have three fundamental responsibilities: They craft a vision, they build alignment, and they champion execution."**
>
> **Anonymous**

MONITORING AND CONTROLLING

In parallel with the execution phase, you, as the business owner and the project manager of your venture, have to monitor and control everything you have planned. Monitoring and controlling will ensure things are being appropriately executed to the standards you have been shooting for in a given project.

You cannot just give your designs to the printing house and leave, only to realize at the end of printing that the printing house has selected the wrong colors and the low paper quality.

You cannot leave your staff to buy the required chemicals from unknown sources with unknown expiry dates and end up with an inferior quality product.

You also have to monitor your spending and your schedule. Project management Performance Indices are used to measure what has been done against what has been planned initially.

For example:

If you have planned that a specific activity will be done in 10 days and cost you 10 dollars, then you realized that the action took only five days and 5 dollars during the execution. Then your Schedule performance Index (SPI) is $10/5 = 2$, and your Cost performance Index (CPI) is also $10/5 = 2$. As long as these indices are more than 1, you are on the safe side. Simple, right?

I am reiteration here that you don't have to memorize these project management indicator unless you are willing to buy or sell businesses. Investors love to hear such expressions because they give them the confidence that they are not working with an amateur.

CLOSING
"Forget what hurt you in the past, but never forget what it taught you."

Shannon L. Alder

Some people think that this phase is the least important among all of the stages mentioned above, but trust me when I tell you that it is not less important than the execution phase.

Closing is the process where you ensure that everything has been entirely done to the standards you have planned for in the planning phase. It means that you have checked list all your requirements and documented lessons learned from the execution phase. Remember, Closing, always help you in your next venture, which you will start shortly after your first successful endeavor.

For example: if you have purchased some inferior quality chemicals from one store, you can register this in your lessons learned repository to not be fooled again with such kinds of deceptions.

I remember a project that I did many years ago manufacturing baseball bats. Baseball bats were the ultimate self-protection weapon in Egypt back in 2011 during the revolution. I subcontracted a carpenter to assemble 100 pieces every day. The venture was quite a success. The only constrain that I did not plan for is the transportation of this massive product. I did not recognize that 100 high-quality baseball bats are heavy to the extent that I need a truck to transport them. When I compare transporting baseball bats with carrying hundreds of 10 ml fragrance bottles that almost sell with the same value, I will prioritize starting with the perfume venture before baseball bats.

OPERATION PHASE

After successfully executing your idea as a Project, you will end up with a high fidelity product you want to start selling. Sales is the bloodstream of the business; you will find much information on the art of sales and marketing in the second part of the book.

ACTUAL EXECUTION
BRANDING (PROJECT PHASE)

"A brand is the set of expectations, memories, stories, and relationships that, taken together, account for a consumer's decision to choose one product or service over another."

Seth Godin

Branding is the name of the game. What you may have realized that we are swimming in a gigantic ocean of brands that surround us everywhere; each has its own USP "unique selling proposition," which screams that I am a better product than my rivals.

Right now, put aside this book and look around you and try to list the number of brands surrounding you.

Look to your watch, your shirt, your jeans, the cup of coffee you are drinking (even if it is home-brewed, indeed it has a brand), the fragrance you are wearing, the soap you washed your hands with, the television you are watching, the laptop you are using. Infinite number is no exaggeration.

Brands were invented to ensure quality and indicate the origin of the product to be consumed. Still, people buy brands to reflect their unique personality, intelligence, Riches, loyalty to a country, or even to a political party.

Companies know this very well and studied how they can provoke such expressions in their customers to keep them buying more and more products from their end.

I am sure you can associate positive emotions with mentioning brands like Rolex, Mercedes, BMW, Apple, Samsung, etc.

Now, you can see companies like Coca-Cola spend 80% of its resources on advertising, and all its ads will reflect these emotions mentioned above and associate them with the brand name.

Soap, insecticides, detergents, perfumes, coffee, breath fresheners, ice cream, junk food, thousands of products labeled with different appealing brands that rely 100% on marketing their unique selling propositions.

Let's interpret some underlining messages for each product unique selling proposition and know what it means:

Detergents: Mother caring for her lovely children and preventing diseases (Family Love)

Fragrance: expression of masculinity or femininity (sex)

Coffee: Professionalism, proactivity (sense of intelligence)

Junk food: Youth

Just give yourself some time to think of your brand's name, logo, and slogan; who knows, maybe your brand will be a global one after a few months.

Note: don't restrict your brand to a specific niche. For example, I have selected "Intellifields" as the brand of my products because it can be used in almost all physical products, and it can also be used in software development.

SELECTING THE PROPER PACKAGE (PROJECT PHASE)

You have a multitude of choices here—shape, size, material, color, etc. Just keep in mind that sometimes the package itself sells because of its high fidelity.

I remember one product that impressed me made by the world's largest chemical company, "DuPont," a cockroach bait gel called "Advion." DuPont put the bait in a syringe! Yes, Syringe with a simple label design. Syringe will make the application of the bait much easier in the cracks and crevices. Their choice of untraditional package, in addition to the product's superiority, made their product the number one selling product in the US market.

Remember, this book's title is repackaging and grow rich; you have to always keep in mind that what will make your product different from the competition is the package and design.

LABEL DESIGN (PROJECT PHASE)
You need an appealing cover with a unique slogan, reflecting your product's ultimate use, such as RoachBuster for Insecticide, **** Oil for fragrance, and Rat Last Meal.

I know you might say this label looks cheap; still, it made me a decent amount of money.

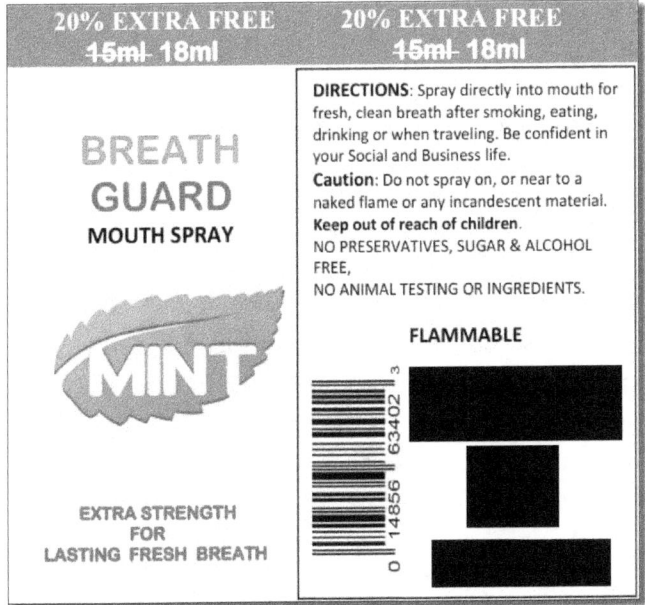

Keep in mind that this step is one of the most critical steps in your business because people adore the brand name, cover design, signs, and logos, and I would instead not risking my first venture by amateurish designing. When talking in terms of designing, you have to remember one statement: the title of #1 bestselling book **"Good to Great,"** your design must be great, not good.

"When Quality is the same, packaging Matters."

"If you're going to do something, try to be the best in the world at it, and if you fail, at least you'll know that you tried"

John Danaher

To hit my point, if you have access now to the internet, please write "Cat litter" in Google's search bar and see the different packages for the same product and how much influence the package design will have to attract the customers. I chose Cat litter because it is a very cheap product to make, yet you can find many price differences between manufacturers. Is it the ingredients? Maybe. Or is it the design of the package?

You can hire a designer and pay extra money to make something tangible, yet I recommend that you exert more effort and design your packages yourself. You can watch designing tutorials on YouTube using the most powerful designing software, which is Adobe Illustrator. You will understand the difference between vector drawing (line drawing) and raster images (pixel images that can be only edited by software like Adobe Photoshop).

I remember when I designed a product label, which happened to be a pepper spray (Red Chilli and preservative, by the way). I used Microsoft Word, the design was horrible, yet I made decent profits from this venture. I think if I have improved the label design, I would have realized better profits then.

	Caution during prototyping

During prototyping, try not to overexpose your product, especially to people that may leak your idea to potential rivals. The road to hell is paved with good intentions. People are obsessed with telling other people stories of success & failure. they will always share your idea with other people and tell them the magic sentence, "please don't tell anybody."

> **"Three may keep a secret if two of them are dead."**
> **Benjamin Franklin**

I know you may be laughing right now because you underestimate this, but that what has indeed happened to me while I was prototyping a fragrance product. The package, label, brand, and everything else has been imitated in a copy-paste manner. Unfortunately, the knockoff's quality was too bad to sell; still, it ruined the market.

You may underestimate your product only to realize later on that this product had a great potential to be a market superstar

Additionally, Beware of printing houses. While you are printing your labels, try to protect the design from leakage, as many rivals make some sort of market studies contacting such printing houses. (Unfortunately, I learned this the hard way too).

NEVER IMITATE
"There are imitators, and there are originators."

Many people think that the best way to start realizing profits is to make knockoffs or copycat a product. Those market wasters hurt authentic product producers, but they also broke themselves by having a short life span of their work.

You are reading this book to make something novel, something expressing your uniqueness. Never resort to such zero-sum games.

Markets need new products to compete against existing ones to reduce prices and improve quality. In that sense, introducing new products to the market improves the economics of a given industry.

"It is better to fail in originality than to succeed in imitation."
Herman Melville

START PROTOTYPING (PRE-OPERATION)

I again invite you to read the book **"Ready, Fire, Aim"** by **Michael Masterson.** In project management, they called this approach of development "Agile" sometimes; it is called iterative. Still, it is all about following a vital sequence to ensure that your product will sell at the end of the day.

Prototyping means that in the very early stages of your business development, you should produce a primitive version of your product (sometimes it is the final version) to test the waters of the market. When you have a real physical product in your hands, you can see and feel the potential market's feedback and receive priceless tweaks from their end to further improve the product. Maybe the packaging is weird and unrecognizable, or the efficacy of the product is compromised. Perhaps the brand name is not attractive.

Maybe the price is not right. The list of probabilities is endless.

Additionally, prototyping safeguard you from losing hundreds, sometimes thousands of dollars on failed products. Since I am a chemist, I term prototyping as the PH meter of the product. It instantaneously gives you an indicator of the success or failure of a subject product or better gives you the required adjustments to be incorporated to reach success and sales.

NOT READY YET
Do not procrastinate; if you selected your niche, done the feasibility, have the material, developed the design, you don't have to wait until everything is perfect.

Remember, Bill Gates started to sell windows 3.1, which kept crashing every few hours but didn't wait until its perfection. People did like it and gave him the support and chance to improve it. Systematically windows reached its excellent position now, making Bill Gates the richest man in the whole world.

IF YOU LIKE IT, BUY IT
It is crucial to know that you need no verbal gratification in the world of business. Many of your closest family members and friends will give you reactions of admiration for your smartness. This could be deceiving because you need to know whether the product will sell or not. So, always try to sell your product for money and never collect feedbacks only. The success of a venture is always measured by how much money you generate from it. That is the only measure of the extent of your success.

Think of it like a football match; many times, you hear that team XYZ played better than their rival; still, in the end, the other team won the game because they have scored goals. Football victory is measured by goals, not by performance.

I know a friend who made $1 million selling his prototype just because of this simple tip. All that he did is to ask people to buy his business. He spent his time collecting opinions and doing market surveys.

> "Ask, and it will be given you. Seek, and you will find. Knock, and it will be opened for you. For everyone who asks receives. He who seeks finds. To him, who knocks, it will be opened."
>
> Matthew 7:7

DON'T RECITE YOUR STORY

Some of your customers commit their purchases to well-known brands, and once they know that you have assembled a product by yourself, they will subconsciously reject to buy it. As the saying goes: **"loose lips sink ships,"** just sell your product, don't recite your development story. Sometimes, it is better for you even not to tell others that the product is yours. Act as if you are a sales representative.

HOW MUCH TO SPEND PROTOTYPING

It depends on your feasibility study. Some prototypes require some money. For example, I have prototyped a baseball bat for $10/piece and prototyped a fragrance roll-on for $1/piece. I believe you are only allowed to spend a maximum of $200 no more; spending more than this is the perfect recipe for disaster.

Note: the expenses of prototyping will be offset by selling such prototypes. So, don't panic. Maybe the income from selling a single piece of your prototypes will make you breakeven (the best ventures I have done followed the infinite return on investment, as we will see later).

MORE THAN ONE PRODUCT

You don't have to make five different products' prototypes in one shot. You would rather sell your most probably successful product prototype first to boost your faith in what you are doing. This will further improve the other products' plans, and you will gain priceless knowledge selling your first-star product in the market. Also, this will relieve you financially while you are kicking off your first business ventures.

REGISTER

Many people think that the hassle of registering a product will put their energy down and deteriorate the whole venture. Part of this is right, I tried many times to register different products, and you won't imagine the amount of obstacles that faced me until I finished the task. Still, nothing is far more pleasurable than owning your product with your brand name written on it.

Registering your product will give you a lot of freedom to publicly advertise and expose your products on others' shelf spaces or through the internet, which is the ultimate leverage for any business. But remember, never register a product before prototyping. Always think in terms of money and time before registration in order not to regret it.

START MARKETING AND SELLING (OPERATION PHASE)

At last, you have your high-end product ready for marketing and sales.

As defined by Wikipedia, "Marketing is profitably using the results of studying short-term and long-term needs of those who can pay for a one-time, or in most cases, a steady flow of service or product placement. In 2017 The New York Times described it as "the art of telling stories so enthralling that people lose track of their wallets."

You have already done your homework, producing your first superstar product, and know very well your targeted markets. You should focus your efforts on promoting your product and aggressively selling it. You have to sell your product extensively in the first few months of production as we will later know that this is an advantage "Being the first one in the marketplace."

> **"If you don't sell, it's not the product that's wrong; it's you."**
> **Estee Lauder**

Sales is the bloodstream of any business. From the very first hours of your venture, you have to start thinking of sales and start selling the prototypes/products to put food on the plate for your family and yourself, not tomorrow, but now.

If you started to think only in terms of marketing, branding, accounting, and other side things at this critical stage of the business "startup," you will just ruin the opportunity.

Sales also give a fast indicator of whether things are moving on in the right direction or not.

Selling is the primary element that can move any business's

gears, whether it is well managed or not. Show me a super manager and super managed company without sound sales, and I can assure you that it will soon declare bankruptcy. Conversely, show me super sales figures and inferior management of a venture, and I can assure you that things will move on, and poor management will soon be spotted and substituted with better ones.

WHEN SHALL I START SELLING?

Immediately. The earlier the venture produces money, the more profitable the whole project's overall economics will be. The funds that will be generated from sales will be reinvested in the same venture or other investments.

SALESFORCE

Here we are talking about the superstars of your successful business story. People have always debated about selling, whether it is a talent or an acquired skill. I can tell you from my experience that there are talented people in selling. They have those innate qualities for sales without receiving any former education or training.

In the book **"The tipping point" by Malcolm Gladwell**, he recognized three types of people who can make viral sales and marketing: Connectors – Market Mavens – Salesmen

- Connectors are those people who have robust networks of friends and acquaintances. If you are happy about having hundreds of friends on Facebook, connectors have hundreds of thousands. Those people can make your product goes viral instantaneously.

- Market Mavens are those people who know everything about products and can make comparisons and give you a detailed review of the pros and cons of one product vs. the other. You have to win their goodwill to make sure that they good mouth your product in front of the many people who ask for their advice.

- Salespeople, of course, are those who make their living selling products professionally. Salespeople are highly motivated when they have superstar products because they will be able to sell more with such products, and hence they will receive more commissions and increase their income.

You have to have a plan connecting to all of the above mentioned to have maximum exposure to the potential markets. You should keep in mind also that your business is infinite networking. You should become the best salesman in your team.

UNIQUE SELLING PROPOSITIONS OR "USP"

You have to have a unique selling proposition or USP to convince your customers why they would buy your product instead of the competition. Give yourself and the whole team the time to enumerate your product's advantages and ensure that the entire team knows them very well.

CUSTOMER IS KING

People are treasures that are buried under a thick cover that has to be dug. If you are willing to make fortunes, you have to keep in mind that people are the sole source of your wealth.

Customer satisfaction is the alpha and omega goal of any business. One customer's joy means your business's positive viral marketing to the customer's family, friends, and acquaintances. The dissatisfaction of one customer is the contagious bad-mouthing of your product to the same people.

So when approaching, Customers always keep in mind the virtual slogan "I am important" above their heads. The rule mentioned in one of the most popular business books **"How to win friends and influence people." By Dale Carnegie.**

BUSINESS STRATEGIES AND SHORTCUTS
OUTSOURCING
"Master your strengths, outsource your weaknesses."

Ryan Khan

One day, one of my friends told me that he is interested in starting a liquid soap factory. He asked me about the soap ingredients, which I didn't hesitate to share the same with him.

Notwithstanding this, I told him instead of manufacturing liquid soap himself, he could search for an existing reputable liquid soap factory and negotiate with them to buy their base soap in bulk at a much lower price than manufacturing it himself.

Then he can innovate on this base soap, whether by adding disinfectants, color, or fragrance, then rebranding the product and charge extra money for it. In such a sense, he reduced the production cost and had the opportunity to prototype and check his new product's market appetite.

That is another approach to own your own business by outsourcing whatever products you need in bulk, then directly repackage it or slightly modifying it.

PARTNERSHIP
One time, I started a breath freshener project (Diluted peppermint oil + food-grade color). I knew that it is illegal to market such a product without registering it.

One of my friends told me that it is easier to make a Joint Venture (JV) "partnership" with a pharmaceutical company than to build your factory from scratch to apply for the required licenses.

In that sense, I signed an NDA "Non-disclosure Agreement" with a reputable Pharmaceuticals Company. I started negotiating the idea openly; afterward, we signed an MOU "Memorandum of Understanding," which defines how we will cooperate until we reach an agreement to sign a Joint Venture Agreement.

Partnership is a powerful business strategy and a shortcut to build on the shoulders of the giants.

"if you can't defeat them, join them."

Refer to Appendices 1, 2 & 3 enclose the Non-Disclosure Agreement "NDA," Memorandum of Understanding "MOU," and Joint Venture Agreement "JVA" templates at the end of this book.

For the partnership mentioned above, there are a lot of approaches to succeed and receive substantial financial gains from such a relationship:

1- JV in a new company with an equity portion by investing your own money (become a shareholder);
2- Convince your partner(s) to have an equity portion as a reward for your ideas and business development efforts (also become a shareholder without hard cash);
3- Sell your business idea and development plans for the giant company and exit.

Note: to convince potential investors like the above mentioned; it takes more than presenting an idea. A properly drafted business plan with preliminary financial indicators will reflect how original your idea is, compared to just talking.

I have also enclosed a high-level Business Plan Guidelines in Appendix 4 that I have followed in negotiating potential business cooperation with one of the largest investors. You have to read it and pay special attention to its structure and the message it conveys.

Such high-level documents are necessary to introduce a potential business opportunity to large investors. It acts as an executive summary that hits the idea straight to the point. If the investor asks for further elaboration, you should take this vital document to the second stage.

The good news is that you have already put the detailed business plan; all you have to do is put additional details to every point you have highlighted previously. You can include risk management plans, further elaboration on the available markets, execution plan and business model, etc.

OPM & OPT LEVERAGES
Other People's Money (OPM)
If you have a successful business confirmed by prototyping and want to quickly upscale it, relying on savings won't be a good idea to finance such upscaling. Sometimes you have to enter the market fast to seize an opportunity, and there is no luxury of time to wait to amount the needed capital. In such cases, the best partner to have is a lender. You can finance your business using Other People's Money (OPM). The rich need to invest their money in safe businesses that can provide them with returns on the sum invested; otherwise, depreciation will slowly wipe their savings. That's where your business comes in. Professionally presenting your feasibility study (not just an idea) to such lenders is the most crucial

step. As the saying goes, **"first impressions last forever."** You have to impress the lenders and make them in a desperate need to venture with you.

BANKS VS. PERSONS

Banks have no emotions involved; all they need is a checklist of eligibility that you have to fulfill to receive the money. On the other hand, capitalists are people with emotions, and they will always want to put their unique touch on any business. Hence I would recommend dealing with banks directly.

Banks are only after receiving their money back with the agreed interest, nothing more or less.

Many people are afraid of banks due to the horror stories of foreclosures and bankruptcies recited whenever banks are mentioned in front of them. Our case here is different, you did your homework, and you followed a plan and an execution scheme to ensure your venture's success. Any negative thing that could happen will be considered as a force majeure "sometimes called the Acts of God," which no one has any influence on. Fortunately, any agreement includes a force majeure article that defines what happens if such things occur (God Forbid).

With our attitude of "Measuring Twice and Cutting Once" and Prototyping, you will minimize the risks because you already have records of your niche and know your business very well.

Some people will tell you that banks will always ask for collateral against the loan granted to you. This is wrong; many banks and lending organizations base their operations on "project finance" and require no guarantees. The process to be granted such project finance is challenging, yes, but the rewards are substantial.

Why substantial? Let me explain by an example:

Imagine now that you have invested $100 of your money buying a perfume. You sold this perfume to a lady for $200. Now, what is your return on investment (ROI)?

Anyone will answer; it is a 100% return. In other words, you duplicated your money in such a transaction.

Great, I want you now to imagine a different scenario. Imagine that you have invested the same $100, but now you have borrowed it temporarily from your dad, and you did precisely as the deal mentioned above, you sold the perfume for $200. Then you gave your dad his money back ($100 - the time of the transaction was instantaneous and didn't require any interest to be paid to your dad), and you have $100 in your pocket. The question now is, what is your return on investment (ROI)?

I am amazed at the number of people who answer this second question and say 100% return. What they don't know is that their answer is gravely wrong. The ROI of this new transaction is infinite simply because you have created something out of nothing. You made $100 out of thin air. Because you didn't put a penny in, but you relied on other people's money, and that is the power of leverage.

Is it smart action? Yes. Is it a risk? Sure, yes, but with intelligent management and carefulness, I can assure you that you could make miracles with this single piece of knowledge. It is truly an unfair advantage that works in your favor.

Note: for the transaction mentioned above relying on borrowing, if you gave the lender an interest, even if it is a substantial bloody interest, you still fulfill the infinite return on investment because a single cent will be created out of the blue.

Typically, banks will ask you to put a down payment or an equity portion to ensure that you are committed to your business.

Sometimes the leverage ratio goes as far as 10%:90% equity to debt, respectively; still, banks will charge more interest for such huge leveraged deals. Again if your numbers are right and your business is solid, you have nothing to lose, and you have everything to gain from such a win/win partnership.

You have to start googling the hell out of your local banks to see which banks are the most eligible to finance your venture with the terms and conditions you find most suitable for you and your partners (if any).

Other People's Time (OPT)

If you are an employee, you should know that you are trading your time with money.

We went to school, then college, some of us gone beyond that and made Masters Degrees and PhDs to be more and more professional. Professional here means that you are specialized in specific fields that contribute to a whole system's success. The more skilled you are, the more you will be rewarded financially.

All of us need professionals in our lives for life to move on. Can you imagine a world without engineers, accountants, pharmacists, chemists, nurses, physicians, mechanics? Of course not.

During your journey, you will need professionals with better knowledge and abilities than yours to facilitate your work. Those devoted individuals will help you in your journey toward riches.

One of my ventures required a lot of physical work filling and sealing bottles, then putting on many labels. I hired three workers who labored day and night in this regard. Ironically, I sold the product for 200X and gave each one 1X, and they were thrilled to receive such wages for the few hours labored.

Of course, I didn't rip them off; we have already agreed on the compensation value even before they have started.

In this venture, I understood the difference between the boss's compensation and that of the employees. Yes, it is brutal, but this is the conscious decision people choose for their lives.

Because you were an employee one day, you should always think of your employees as business partners because they labor day and night for your success, although their compensation is minimal. As I have mentioned before, your sales team is your primary asset; you should treat them fairly and never lose their goodwill.

CASE STUDY
Disinfectants

"The two most important requirements for major success are: first, being in the right place at the right time, and second, doing something about it."

Ray Kroc

Nothing is more powerful than finding the right product at the right time. I am sure the outbreak of COVID-19 made some millionaires instantly. Do you know why I am confident about this? Because those millionaires came to me asking for help regarding the labels of their disinfectant packages.

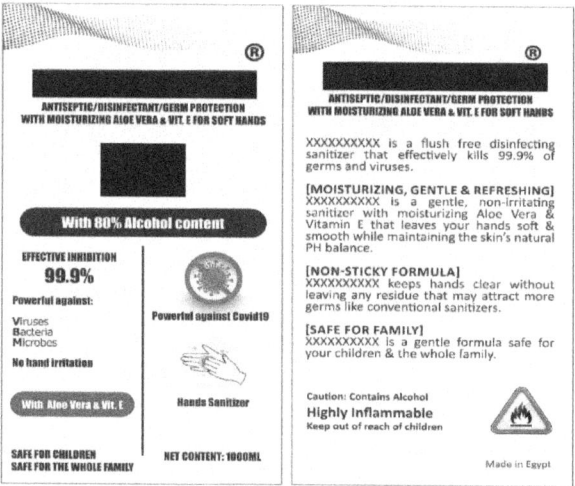

Those successful people didn't hesitate and didn't overthink producing and marketing their brand of disinfectant.

Others were concerned about the quality of the alcohol used, its concentration, whether to add color or not, whether to add moisturizers or not, never-ending reasons not to start production and selling.

A friend of mine chose the right plastic package, secured a decent amount of alcohol, and started designing the labels in 24 hours.

Fortunately, as we all have witnessed, governments supported hand sanitizers' supply even through black markets, and my friend marketed his products even to the governmental officials.

As we have mentioned earlier, many people said this is unfair or unethical to build fortunes out of other people's misfortunes and need. These are nonsense because my friend and many others were selling their products at a fair price, and customers didn't complain.

All that those smart and active people did is fill a gap in the market, and they have been rewarded generously.

On the other hand, some people were innovative; they open a blue ocean by stepping out of the competition.

Ordinary producers were seeking the same principle raw material of disinfectants, which is alcohol. The smarter producers who have the unfair advantage of knowledge (they did some homework) knew a wide array of disinfectants available from the local market.

One of the most potent disinfectants is Hydrogen Peroxide. Unlike bleach, Hydrogen Peroxide decomposes to give pure oxygen and water, which are both non-toxic. Hence, the products relying on this substance could be easily marketed to companies in bulk to disinfect offices and clean floors.

Other smarter guys introduced the idea of nano-copper sprays that are being sprayed on face masks to disinfect their surfaces and last for longer times than alcohol and other products.

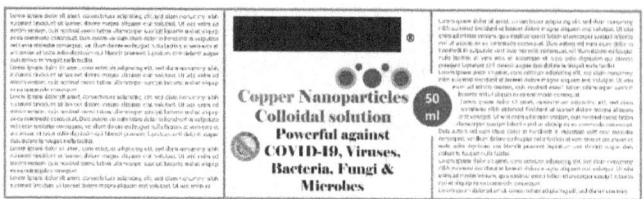

Note: Nano-Copper could be easily manufactured by dissolving ascorbic acid (Vitamin-C) in a Copper Sulfate solution. You know that Vitamin-C is an antioxidant; hence it reduces Copper ions to elemental Copper but in a minimal size, which is suitable for spraying on surfaces. It is not rocket science, isn't it?

I know you may have some fears about quality here, but I rest assured you that if you are going to let your parents and beloved ones use your product, you should market and sell your product confidently without hesitation. If not, then you should consider optimizing it to reach the extent of using it yourself.

Similarly, nano-silver could be manufactured the same way, and the same has similar antiviral and antibacterial properties that could be useful in fighting infections during these challenging times.

PART 2

SAVE A LITTLE MONEY FOR A RAINY DAY

Two factors contribute to anyone's financial success: the first is the amount of money you can generate, and the second is how much of this generated money you can keep.

Saving is your insurance policy against the unknown, or it is a building block for more money to generate. Every penny saved today can, later on, contribute to the success of your endeavors in the future.

Sometimes we underestimate the power of saving and just spend the extra bucks here and there on useless things. We don't know that these extra bucks can become the seed of millions of dollars if they are invested well.

Generally, ordinary people cannot hold the temptation of spending to show other people that they are rich. Hence, they buy irrationalities. While their cellphones are perfectly functioning, they lust for the new cellphone with these extra features that they will never use during their lifetime. The same goes for desktops, watches, laptops, vehicles, and the list is endless. Instead of looking at the gadgets' utilitarian side, they just buy to satisfy their sense of worthiness.

Sometimes we think that we will be happier if we spend more, a case called "emotional spending," and the result is that we end up compiling vast amounts of literal "useless junk." Sometimes, if the gadgets' price was too high, the reverse happens, and post-purchase depression strikes.

We have to cultivate the habit of saving; we have to stop the ruthless spending addiction that will destroy our future life.

One day, I was sitting with a coffee shop owner discussing some business issues when a waiter came to take our orders. I ordered my regular double espresso as a start to boost my caffeine levels. Ironically, the cafe owner brought out of his pocket a tea bag (like that we use in our homes) and handed it to the diligent waiter! I just stared at him with surprise; how come the owner of a café brings his tea or coffee with him? What a stingy person he is?

He told me that he is saving these extra bucks to be spent wisely on other important things! Can you believe this? A lot of people will reject this idea of excessive frugality. Sometimes they term it stinginess, but you know what?

I saw this same person giving off for the sake of charity an insane amount of money daily.

Again, this is not an invitation to parsimony; it is an invitation to wisdom and frugality; you have to keep records of your spending by knowing your expenditures. Once you do so, you will spot which spending is right and which is wrong.

There are two ways to amount wealth; the first way by creating money; the second way is by saving it. It won't make any sense if you made millions of dollars per year, and you spend them all on whatever reason you spent them on. It resembles those who have won the lottery and became mad spending on ridiculous things until they return to where they were before the lottery, sometimes worse.

If you followed the rules of part 1 and started to generate more income, you should save this money and reinvest it until you pioneer the game's secrets.

DON'T CONFORM TO THE STATUS QUO

Since our childhood, we were taught to conform. We were taught to follow the rules at school, at college, and even at work. The problem is by conformity; we will end up mediocre like everyone else. It is said that some people are following the rules and others make the rules. It is your call to choose which side you want to be now as this is a conscious decision you have to make as early as possible. It is never too late to make such a decision. I can assure you that you can recover a part of your life that has been wasted following the herd with such a decision.

We were created to think, not to follow, and to create rather than imitate.

"If you can't win by being better, you can win by being different."

Remember, we make our habits, then our habits make us. Thinking is a habit that you have to cultivate. Give yourself at least 1 hour per day, preferably early in the morning, to think.

Ask yourself thought-provoking questions like, how can I increase my income today? How can I solve such and such problems? Will solving a particular problem pay off? Can I register my solution so that I can gain monetary compensation for my efforts?

You should think outside the box, as the saying goes. You don't want to end up a retiree dependent on government support until the day you die.

PUSHING BEYOND THE BOUNDARIES

"In order to have what you have not, you must do what you do not."

Albert Einstein defined insanity as doing the same things again and again and expecting a different result. Suppose you kept trapped in your comfort zone (employment) and kept being addicted to the monthly paycheck. In that case, you will end up as a retiree relying on a diminished monthly pension, which won't fulfill your needs, especially at old age.

Watch and observe the retirees around you and ask yourself a question: Do you want to be like them when you grow older? Do you want to be at the same level financially? If your answer is yes, you should not risk starting your own business and focusing solely on your day job to climb the corporate ladder and achieve success there. If your answer is no, and it is expected that it will be so because you are reading this book. Then you have to stop wasting time and start moving forward with your full potential. Keep nagging for success, day and night, never quit, and never give up.

The more you exert effort thinking of ideas and solutions to your problems and others' problems, the more the chance of your success. Just do not give up quickly if things take a little bit more time than you were expecting. You should know that you train your mental muscles the same way as you train your normal muscles in a gym. First, you will find things hard, but afterward, you will lift weights you have never imagined to lift it before.

As the saying goes: **"If you're able to do what needs to be done even with an unmotivated mind, you're a definite winner."**

Training your mental muscles requires many untraditional activities that you should do daily in order not to lose momentum. You should be an avid reader, reading books related to business development and entrepreneurship. You should consider all things around you literally as business opportunities, observe your surroundings and search for a tweak here and another there until you find something with potential. The keywords here are **Open your eyes & Observe!**

While I am writing these words, I remember the well-known story titled "Acres of Diamonds" by Russell H. Conwell, which in summary narrates the story of an African farmer who saw other people mining for diamonds and realizing substantial profits. He didn't hesitate to sell his farm, took the money, and searched for diamonds, unfortunately with no luck. In the end, he committed suicide, throwing himself in the river. On the other hand, the guy who bought his farm observed many glimmering stones while diligently working to raise crops. One day, a friend of his told him that the glimmering stones are diamonds, and the farm is full of them.

The moral of the story: "You don't have to search for success and happiness anywhere external. All your dreams, opportunities, fulfillment, and happiness could be found where you live."

Keep working diligently until "bad luck" fed up with you and let you go.

STOP PROCRASTINATION

Procrastination is your real enemy in this adventure. Don't wait until everything is ready. If you didn't take a step today, someone else would do.

Puzzlingly, by some kind of supernatural power, other people will distinguish your idea, plan its execution, and start it. The same has happened again and again. You can verify this by searching the number of ideas that two or more people have thought about simultaneously. You will be amazed by the numbers.

I believe the world tosses ideas in the skies and awaits the receiver. If the receiver didn't show up, others would do.

Start for God's sake, at least start searching for new ideas, put a plan, gather information, but start. Once you start, you will find things snowballing.

> **"Procrastination is the bad habit of putting off until the day after tomorrow what should have been done the day before yesterday."**

Napoleon Hill

PROVIDE VALUE

Many of us are tempted to make money without caring, whether what we provide has added value to customers. You don't want to fall into this trap of inventing useless stuff to make a few bucks.

Fortunately, people are not stupid; they recognize scammers and punish them brutally by word of mouth epidemics or reviews. I can assure you once a fake businessman is blacklisted, there is no room for him anymore to re-enter the market.

Luckily, you are free to think of any ideas, and you can select the most beneficial ones for your customers to start your venture with. In such a sense, you will build a reputation of authenticity, and customers will be happy to do business with you in this venture and other future ones.

A simple test you can do to ensure that you are providing value, put yourself in other people's shoes. Would you be happy to use or consume the product or service you intend to invent? Would you be glad to buy similar products in the future and commit to the same brand?

I remember buying a GPS software from one of the reputable companies to find that the same is loaded with hidden paid plugins required to make the software functional. I got angry and swore that whenever the same company is mentioned in front of me, I will share my bad experience to take my revenge.

> "How do you know what people value? Well, you watch what they buy. How do we know what products to create? Well, it's based on what they value."
>
> Peter Senge

BE THE FIRST ONE IN THE MARKET PLACE

If you introduced something unique to the market, something with no resemblance, you would have an unfair advantage of monopoly for a maximum of 4 months. Yes, only four months until you start competing against imitators and market ruiners. The good news is that in this limited time, is you can amount fortunes if you did your homework correctly. In such time, you have to maximize your sales, never look to product optimization or any other managerial aspects—just full-throttle sales.

Fortunes are only made on such occasions. I can assure you about that.

INTRODUCE SOMETHING NOVEL

Many so-called entrepreneurs think that imitating products or services with a bullish market is the right business approach. They act just like those trading on the stock market on a day-to-day basis, a category called "flippers." The problem with flippers is that they are market-driven; if the market is bullish, they buy if the market is perishing, they sell. This means that they are governed by circumstances as if they are in the vehicle's driven seat where they do not influence at all. As you may have read, such people end up doing nothing. Some of their portfolio investments go up, and the other goes down, and the net result is zero.

The same is valid with imitators. They play a copycat game in a late stage of a product or a service lifecycle, leading to a very short lifetime of business and profits. Very soon, the number of copycats will increase exponentially, leading to a perish drift down the hill in the market, making all those so-called investors or entrepreneurs losers.

On the other hand, if you think of original ideas and original products, you will be deemed an initiator, not an imitator. A position that provides you with an aura of knowledge and novelty that could give you the required reputation needed to boost your business in the early stages of your business lifetime.

I recall the book **"Blue Ocean Strategy" by W. Chan Kim and Renée Mauborgne.** In this book, the authors indicated that you should not compete in the existing markets, which leads to red oceans of blood; instead, think of opening new markets by introducing something novel that puts you out of competition.

> **"Companies aren't families. They're battlefields in a civil war."**
>
> Charles Duhigg

Example: Coca Cola vs. Pepsi is a typical lifelong example of severe competition that leads to a lose/lose relationship.

Dr. Pepper has opened a blue ocean by merely introducing a tweak (cherry coke), which made it a standalone product out of such competition.

Remember, no rocket science is required for you to introduce something novel and unique. The world around you is full of products that need improvement. You could be the one person who has spotted such modification. You had the guts and entrepreneurial qualities to introduce such change to the market, which is desperate for the same.

Note: Whenever I see some people imitate my products or services, I become delighted because people follow me. It satisfies my ego that my original thinking was good enough to grasp those people's attention, especially if they are well off financially.

GATHER OPINIONS

Although we said, **"Loose lips sink ships,"** It doesn't mean that you will never ask for the opinion of others. Your best friends, family members, and spouse can give you priceless opinions about your intended product. Try to sell them the product (you don't have to tell them every nitty-gritty aspect of the project) and just listen to them to know customers' feedback. They can tell you about some modifications at this early development stage that could translate to millions of dollars of profits or reduce the losses by millions of dollars.

But again, be careful disclosing your ideas to rivals or people who don't love you because they will try to put you down or ruin your intended business.

One day, one of my acquaintances told me that he would manufacture his fragrance line, telling me that he will put too much emphasis on quality rather than anything else. I told him I am already in this market, and people love the package more than anything else. If you want to sell your product, you should focus on package design and brand name. Unfortunately, he didn't listen to me and packaged his product in a cheap glass bottle. The perfume was terrific and lasted forever, but it didn't sell. People were passing by his outlets and didn't give themselves a chance to try it. He didn't gather opinions from his friends, and the results were catastrophic.

You have to have this talent of differentiating between authentic, constructive criticism and jealous, destructive condemnation.

> "Every human being is entitled to courtesy and consideration. Constructive criticism is not only to be expected but sought."
> Margaret Chase Smith

IF YOU ARE LOOKING FOR SECURITY...

One day I met a school colleague, and we had a long conversation. He told me that he hates his day job. I told him, why won't you quit and find another job or better start your own business? He simply said that he is enslaved in this job to meet ends and secure all family needs. He told me that he could not imagine the idea of being jobless for a single day. Additionally, he said that if he quit his job now, he will lose a long journey climbing the corporate ladder, and his rivals would celebrate such leave.

The reality is that the most secure place in the world is the jail because there are walls of concrete and rods of Iron that protect you from anything outside. But think about it for a minute; look what you have done to yourself. You may have the capabilities to be something better. You may have the capabilities to contribute to the welfare of humanity. You may have the chance to be richer and healthier. Don't limit yourself to the status quo. This comfort zone is a killer.

The feeling of insecurity is brutal, right? Yes. But it is the motive and fuel that push us away from mediocrity.

As the saying goes: **"where there's a will, there's a way."**

If you are willing to expand your means and live a better life than what you are currently living, you should know that it has a price, and you have to pay for it.

"If you don't pay the price for success, you'll pay the price for failure."
                                                                    Zig Ziglar

BOOTSTRAPPING

Verb

Gerund or present participle: bootstrapping

Get (oneself or something) into or out of a situation using existing resources.

"The company is bootstrapping itself out of a marred financial past."

Bootstrapping is simply to make instead of to buy. Reducing the expenses as much as possible will increase your success as it will increase the profits and reduce the risk of losses if the venture didn't work out.

Some people will say: "there is no such thing as something out of nothing," and they are right. I didn't mean by reducing expenses that you will not pay anything; on the contrary, Your time and effort are both translated to a large amount of money. Just your ideas could be translated to millions of dollars, and this is all what this all about. Remember when you hear the word bootstrapping that Bill Gates and Steve Jobs were programming by themselves, both didn't outsource programmers to do their software or line of products.

Bootstrapping is anything that could be done in-house (by yourself); do it yourself, and don't waste additional money outsourcing it from external sources. For example, designing, if you can use software like Microsoft Powerpoint or Adobe Illustrator, then you have all that you want to design a good looking logo or label.

That's how millions are compiled. If you asked a self-made millionaire about his journey, he would tell you the same.

Your work is to keep thinking of creating businesses that require zero or "few bucks" upfront and that harvests millions of dollars at the end of such venture.

"What's a bootstrapper to do?
You have to go where the other guys can't. Take advantage of what you have so that you can beat the competition with what they don't."

Seth Godin

THE POOR, THE MIDDLE CLASS AND THE RICH.

Sometimes we ask ourselves why some people are rich while others are poor? While we don't know whether we are rich or poor, and we end up as all people thinking that we are "middle class."

Well, this question has long been asked, and many books have professionally addressed it. I will elaborate on the definitions a little bit further in the below diagram:

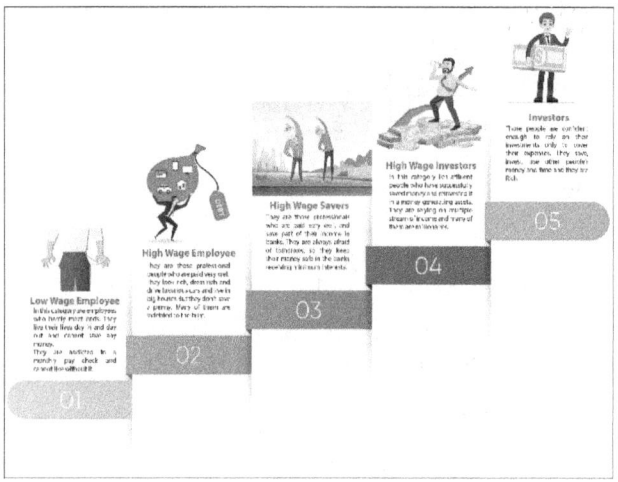

Low Wage Employee

They are those people who are barely meeting ends. They are trapped in the rat race as they have many obligations to be covered. They are working day and night to fulfill the needs of their family. They don't have the luxury to lead an average life like other members of the community. They cannot change their career, and they cannot save from it a penny. Their work does not allow them to advance financially or professionally. Hence, we can consider them as "poor," and sadly, they know it.

High Wage Employee

They are those professionals (well-educated people, having high college degrees) working in prestigious corporations like multinationals, and they are earning respectful salaries. The problem with this category of people that they don't know that they are poor as long as they don't save and invest. They think that they are rich because they are leading a prosperous life. Hence, they spend their money on expensive suits, large homes, and beautiful cars. Many of them are indebted because they are living a life that is not theirs. We can categorize those people as "poor," but they don't know it. Maybe the low wage employees are in a better financial position than them because low wage employees live below their means and know their limits, so they never borrow to spend it on absurdities from their point of view.

If you compare the low and high-wage employees' financial statements, you would recognize that the former is zero, but the latter is below zero.

Another massive problem with this category of people is that they think the only way to become rich is to work harder and longer. This concept has always been preached in the industrial age; unfortunately, they do not know that the same is a disaster recipe. Working day and night will not make you richer; on the contrary, it could damage your health, family, and social life.

High Wage Savers

In this category lies the average person; maybe your father and mine are from this kind of herd. They are professionals who work diligently, and they live below their means. They know that falsely living the rich's lives won't get them anywhere; instead, it can destroy their lives, especially when they most need their money after retirement. Hence, those people work and save part of their monthly paycheck in banks in the form of a certificate of deposits or a saving accounts and receive the minimum interest, which almost balances their currency's inflation rate. Unfortunately, those people start to realize that they have chosen the wrong plan for their lives too late when they are retired. The pension is not like a full working salary, and withdrawing from the life savings tastes brutal. Many people try to invest in ridiculous opportunities, and many fail because they didn't practice investing during their whole lifetime. The advice for those people is to live again below their means.

"To retire is to expire."

High wage investors

In this category are those people who have a plan. They know the high-level strategy of success and richness. Work, save, and invest are their simple but effective plan. Those people know very well that saving without investing is the ultimate failure because they will end up limited, and inflation will eat their savings slowly. On the other hand, investing is a limitless adventure that could lead them to places they have never imagined.

I think this category is the one we want to start shooting for. Working hard is not enough; working hard and saving are not enough too. You have to push a little further and make your money work for you. This is the power of investment. Investing in Real Estate and leasing the property, trading or better start repackaging business as described in part I of this book are all means of investing.

As mentioned above, many people think that the only way to get rich is to work more and work hard. In this category, the slogan is to work less but work smarter. The people in this category know that we have limited abilities and limited time to amount wealth. Hence, they rely on other resources that could leverage their time and skills.

I used to have a small condominium apartment in an excellent neighborhood. The property by which my family has preserved it for me to get married and live in it. One day, I read a book about investment, and I asked myself what would happen if I fully furnished this apartment and start to rent it to high-end tenants.

As you may predict, my parents opposed the idea immediately, telling me all such horrible things as how tenants could damage my property and how some of them may do illegal activities that could subject me to legal problems. Some of them may not pay the rent and on and on. Endless limitations were popping up, and I couldn't believe how creative my parents were coming with all things that might go wrong to convince me.

The Irony is that the book indicated that this would happen. It said that you would find many people, especially family members, oppose the idea of renting the apartment and the reason is obvious because they didn't do it before. That's why I made my mind and decided to venture through, and the results were substantial. I made my first capital in a few minutes, negotiating a good deal with a brit who happened to work near my apartment. For the first time, I tasted the sweetness of passive income, and I knew the power of investing.

The second Irony is that the rent per month was exactly equal in value to the salary I used to earn then. Which immediately meant many things:

I doubled my income, which allowed me to double what I can do with a single income stream.

I could quit my day job (if I want, which I didn't) and still can live the same standard of living I used to live, but now I have the luxury of time to think of new ideas and possibilities that could increase my investment returns and increase my means of living.

I could further save but now faster and reinvest the saved money in a money-generating asset to liberate me from employment slavery.

The possibilities were limitless because I decided to magnify my means.

Did you see the significant difference between the categories mentioned above?

INVESTORS

They are those people who have tasted the sweetness of investment and its power and decided to never return to the slavery of employment.

Such people spend years and years of their lives, investing to the extent that they are no more considering employment as an option. They are no more dependent. On the contrary, those people provide employment opportunities to those who didn't find their path yet. They are improving other people's lives by providing solutions to problems or making life more comfortable through their products and services. They are awesome.

God created us to be in this category. We have to think creatively, create new things, explore new solutions, and provide such utility to our human fellows.

The age is no more a boundary in an investor's face because no more certificates are required to prove that the investor is good enough for a place or a title or have the required physique to perform some duties.

No racism in this category. It does not matter what color, nationality, religion, gender, age, or political party you support. In this category, money only talks and walks.

As the saying goes, **"Business is Business,"** investors are only after one great aim, which is the search for great opportunities to put their money in, watch it multiplying and watch their wealth multiplying with it too.

When your part-time business starts to pay off, you will begin to feel that your daytime job is becoming more and more of a burden on you. It is time for you to become a 100% investor.

Note: It doesn't mean that if you were a low-wage employee that you don't have a chance to be a multimillionaire; on the contrary. You may have a burning desire; other average people have not, and trust me that one of the key aspects of success is to have that killing desire to be successful. I made the classification mentioned above to show you that many people live and die without even knowing what category they are in. the good news is that once you have this knowledge, you choose to select which class you would like to settle there. High wage employees may have a more straightforward adventure as their high paying day job provides them with more chances to try again and again, but low wage employees will follow a measure twice cut once strategy as the money they have saved will be cut from their blood, sweat, and tears.

Note	The mindsets of the Rich, the middle class, and the poor
	It is said that "the Rich think of creating things, the middle class think of circumstances and news, and the poor compare themselves with other people." Don't concern yourself with the circumstances and news you have no influence on them, and never compare yourself with other people. The best way to reach your goal of becoming wealthy is to focus your attention on creating useful things. Thinking of innovative solutions to other peoples' problems is the key to every success you are currently witnessing.

DIVERSIFY

Usually, Well-Informed investors will not risk everything on one endeavor. It doesn't mean that if you have one excellent money-generating asset, it is the time to quit your day job.

No, we want to play it safe here. For you to take that decision, you have to have more than two (2) low-risk money generating assets like:

- ✓ Real Estate rental property that you have signed a long-term contract for its leasing or confident enough that you will be able to rent it if the current tenant left promptly.
- ✓ Owning a car and leasing it to taxi or Uber drivers. This has to be well managed and covered under an adequate insurance policy to ensure the venture's success.

Definitely, for the examples mentioned above, if you have multiples of the same, then you have done a great diversified investment portfolio generally because you are not relying solely on a single investment vehicle.

The assets mentioned above will give you the freedom to think clearly about your upcoming business venture. These assets will generate enough income that could cover your monthly expenses, relieving you from the stress of meeting ends.

To better understand these concepts, I invite you to play a game called **Cashflow 101 and Cashflow 202 made by Robert Kiyosaki, the Rich Dad book series author.** In a nutshell, all you have to do is get out of the "Rat Race" by acquiring many assets that generate passive income until this passive income is equal or exceeds your expenses; At this point, you are free and out of the Rat Race. I know you might think that this is a trivial activity for understanding the whole strategy; Still, I am sure you will not regret it.

SEARCH FOR A MENTOR

A study about Rubik's Cube states that if an average person with no knowledge about any tricks to solve Rubik's cube, it could take him almost 100 years to do so. On the other hand, if the average person sought a mentor (someone who has solved the cube many times and knows all the tricks related to its solving), it would be solved in less than five (5) minutes.

Did you see how important a mentor is?

When people first read the word mentor, the first thing that pops into their minds is a person they have to contact to receive such wisdom. But the reality is an entirely different thing. You can consider this book as a mentor, so as many other wonderful books include all the knowledge, wisdom, tips & tricks, and roadmaps you will want during your journey. Attending seminars, watching video tutorials, and sometimes playing educational games are considered mentors for you.

On the other hand, if you already know a successful business owner or an investor, this is an unfair advantage for you to learn directly from a human-like you. You can invite him or her for a cup of coffee and ask them for advice. You will be amazed at how those people will be willing to support you, especially requesting them generally on how to invest and not asking them about their own business and trade secrets. People love to mentor.

Caution: Select your mentor very carefully because, during your journey, you may find a lot of swindlers and crooks that could waste your time and money. Those evil people adore giving advice and acting as mentors.

You have to know very well the track record of the person that you are going to consult. Don't ever take business consultation from an excellent employee. It is the analogy of wanting to have a good haircut, and you go to the shoemaker because you heard that he is excellent in his job.

Always ask for his or her track record and beware of crooks.

SETTING GOALS

"Success is the progressive realization of a worthy goal."

I won't tell you how important this subject is because, for me, it is everything. We cannot achieve anything without having a well-defined goal. Imagine you entered your car in the morning, started the engine, and drove without a well-defined destination. You will agree with me that you will end up lost. If you didn't recognize a destination for your trip, the fuel would be fully consumed, your money and your energy too will be worn-out, and you will end up nowhere.

It may be a challenging exercise for you to develop a definite goal for your life because you lived all these years long without any, but I invite you right now to calm down and think. What do you want to achieve in your life? Don't tell me I want to be rich. This is not a definite goal because money is a natural byproduct of success. It is the same example of someone telling me that he wants to be happy. Happiness comes when you fulfill or do something that you feel satisfied with, like marrying your beloved one, like raising your children successfully to the social and educational level that you have always dreamed about for them. But you cannot say I want to be happy or prosperous, just don't confuse your internal compass for God's sake.

If you asked me what your goal is in life? I will tell you straight away some prioritized list of goals (not dreams) that I am currently achieving:

1- owning a world-class chemical manufacturing facilities that produce a broad array of products that facilitates people's life. Chemical products like detergents, diapers, soap, antiseptics, antiperspirants, lotions, and much more.
2- From the business mentioned above, I will invest some money in real estate properties that I will rent to provide me with that lovely passive income that will help me and my wife retire without even thinking of actively working again.
3- Reading and writing as freely as I can, and that's the ultimate goal of any wise man. Reading makes you live many lives. Authors put their life-long experiences in a nutshell in a book for you to browse through in a matter of hours, and you are telling me that you are busy doing something else. I don't think so.

I can promise you that miracles will happen to you if you put a big realistic goal for yourself. You will find yourself being attracted to the things that will make you fulfill such a purpose in the shortest time. Additionally, you will find yourself addicted to your new habit of setting goals and reaching them one by one.

Tip	Urgent Vs. Important Matrix
One method to categorize or prioritize your life's most critical tasks is to follow the urgent vs. the important matrix. The rule is simple to make a 3x3 table like the following:	

Items	Important	Not important
Urgent	Do First • Respond to an important email • Go to the dentist to fix your tooth	Delegate • Paying bills • Buy groceries
Not Urgent	Schedule This includes the most critical block you should focus on to get the most out of your life. • Reading books; • Working out; • Thinking of new business ideas.	Delete • Respond to Facebook comments; • Watching movies; • Surfing the internet aimlessly;

You should update this table every day and keep it in front of you to know what matters most in your life.

The urgent, important things are that you have to work in a hurry, and they are very short-term things (e.g., finishing a vital document to be submitted to an official).

The urgent and non-important are the normal every day to day distractors. Every day is full of such things; you could use the tricks mentioned before. The best solution for these activities is to delegate such activities

to authorized persons capable of executing them.
Important and not Urgent things are those essential things that could make a significant difference in your life. Working on a certificate like the Project Management Professional (PMP) was one of my Important - Not Urgent tasks that, by achieving it, filled many gaps in my knowledge and career. Finding technical solutions to a global problem is another important and not urgent task. These are Noble Prize-winning activities that could dramatically change people's lives.

Not Important and Not urgent, these are the tasks that you must remove entirely from your life—browsing the internet aimlessly, excessive gaming, excessive social media browsing, befriending the wrong dudes. You have to succeed in weeding out such tasks altogether from your life to succeed.

Time is all that we have in common with all people walking the earth right now, whether they are ultra-rich or not; spend it wisely like successful people do, and I can assure you that success will be readily granted to you.

WHAT YOU THINK ABOUT YOU BRING ABOUT

It has long been stated in all religions and all philosophical citations that **"We become what we think about."**

What we think about here is not a matter of just momentarily thinking, as many of us might think. We are talking here about deep belief in ourselves that we will succeed and make something tangible. Such deep faith has to become religiously embedded in our hearts and minds to become a reality.

You may have read the book **"the secret,"** and you may have known that all what is included there is true. We become what we think of ourselves, nothing more or less.

Everything starts as a thought. Can you believe this? Look around you right now and observe that anything your eyes see must have started as an idea in the mind of someone. All inventions, all advancements in technology and science, and even literature and arts begin as a thought. The question now is, why won't you start thinking and be the next inventor or creator of something beneficial to yourself and humankind.

Imagine one day you woke up and assumed that today would not be a good day. You will find yourself acting in a way to fulfill your prophecy. You may not want to shower because it does not make any sense to wash up for a bad day. You may not comb your hair as well. You will not shave, and definitely, you will not wear something impressive. After doing all of the previously mentioned, you will generally find people looking at you in a criticizing manner; your friends and family members may avoid you, and your prophecy is at last fulfilled. Because you created it and you wanted to prove to yourself that it is true.

On the other hand, if you woke up and assumed that today would be a great day. You will find yourself full of energy and motivation. You will jump out of your bed, shave and shower, wear the best clothes you have, and show up early at your work. People will receive your positive vibes, and the prophecy will again be fulfilled.

WATCHOUT THE VIBES

When we meet motivated people, we feel motivated and cannot wait to do something positive. Motivated people have provided us with positive vibes, as the saying goes. Their frequency is tuned to motivate and uplift themselves and the people around them.

On the other hand, if you contacted a demotivated or unhappy fellow, you will become depressed and demotivated. Sometimes, I called those guys "black holes" as they can suck off your power.

Some religions call this envy and resentment, but I like to be more scientific about it; this is simply the law of sympathetic resonance:

"Sympathetic resonance or sympathetic vibration is a harmonic phenomenon wherein a formerly passive string or vibratory body responds to external vibrations to which it has a harmonic likeness. The classic example is demonstrated with two similar tuning-forks of which one is mounted on a wooden box. If the other one is struck and then placed on the box, then muted, the un-struck mounted fork will be heard. Similarly, strings will respond to the external vibrations of a tuning-fork when sufficient harmonic relations exist between the respective vibratory modes".

Since we are very sophisticated beings, our bodies respond the same way as the tuning forks mentioned above. Upon receiving a positive frequency, we will resonate positively, and the opposite is true.

Hence, it is recommended to avoid the unhappy and unlucky because they are contagious; they can infect you with their negative energy without your recognition.

I mean by unhappy and unlucky those who choose to be so voluntarily although they can choose the opposite. All of us have problems, struggles, and challenges that we need to overcome. Some people face the same with a smile and optimism, while others meet them with depression and criticism. Therefore you have to stay with those champions who decide to smile and laugh in the face of their struggles and avoid like a plague the malicious fellows.

Remember negative attitude will never lead you anywhere. You cannot solve problems by frowning and criticizing, but you can solve your problems by being positive and centered. You have to know when you face a problem that some people out there have faced far much-complicated problems than yours, and they were able to overcome them by being positive and being smart.

In this regard, I invite you to read the book **"How to stop worrying and start living" by Dale Carnegie**, which includes many strategies to overcome worrying and negative thinking.

YOUR FRIENDS

"Show me your friends, and I will show you your future."

Dan Peña

"You are the average of the Five People you spend the most time with."

Jim Rohn

Select those who surround you carefully as they will have much influence on your future and success. You will understand the difference very well when you hang out with entrepreneurs and with average guys. You will know that entrepreneurs have a different dictionary of nouns and verbs than the average guy. You will always hear the typical business keywords **ROI**, leverage, **IRR**, **NPV**, Payback period, etc. On the other hand, the average guy will always talk about football matches, movies, novels, news, family problems, etc.

Another advantage of hanging out with entrepreneurs and successful people is that they will always positively treat you and motivate you. You will also be open to discussing anything with those guys. You are sure that they hold no resentment against you by any means to provide you with authentic advice without any personal interests involved.

I know you might disagree with me if I told you that the best friend I recommend is a book. The book is the only friend who will always be there whenever you want him. He will never be fed up with you. He will always provide you with knowledge and wisdom and will never waste your time.

IT IS NEVER TOO LATE

Many of us say to themselves and their beloved ones, "I am too old doing this or that" or "I should have done this long time ago." The problem with such words is that the youth even recite it. I remember one day, I decided to learn the German language because there were great career opportunities for chemists in Germany. So, I didn't hesitate to browse through the internet and start learning (democratizing the means of production).

I found many free material, videos, audio recordings, and software that could effectively make my task easy. After a few days, I told myself, how could I waste my precious time studying a new language while I am that old? Children and students at school learn such languages early in their lives, and that's it. I told myself, you are just wasting your time.

You know what, years passed now, and I wasted a lot of time in meaningless activities, and I regret not studying German.

Colonel Sanders - Kentucky Fried Chicken founder in 1952, at the age of 65, when most people are looking at slowing down and retiring, began Kentucky Fried Chicken and definitely, you know the result.

IMPACT

Did you ever wonder why movie stars, musicians, singers, and football players receive more considerable sums of money than a school teacher or an engineer working diligently in a field?

Impact is simply how many people will use or be affected by your product or service. Celebrities and football players are famous, and millions, sometimes billions of people worldwide, watch their movies or football matches and are much fascinated by them. You may know that some royalties are being paid to such stars through advertising or percentage of revenue pre-agreed upon between celebrities and the companies promoting their services and products.

When you start thinking at the very beginning of your venture, you should consider impact as a primary element for your success. Trust me, you could create a superstar product but with minimal impact and end up being a failure. You don't want to climb the wrong mountain, as the saying goes.

I would instead introduce a product that is not limited to: gender - age - demographics.

When I started writing this book, I selected the English language as the first edition's primary language. Why didn't I choose the Arabic language instead, although I am a native Arabic speaker? That's because the English language is like the US dollar, it is the universal language, and most people worldwide can read it, which increases the book's impact in the market.

Since I am a chemist, I was excited to write a chemistry book instead of writing a business book. I have vast experience in the field of fertilizers and petrochemicals, and writing a book with such titles shall be a piece of cake. Instead, I chose to distill my business and entrepreneurial experience and put the same in writing as business books have a broader market than chemistry markets.

To put it another way, before spending time, money, and effort creating a product, you should assess the product's market.

ACHIEVEMENT

"Great things are done when men and mountains meet."

William Blake

One of the most beautiful rewards you can experience is the sense of achievement. When you set a goal and start progressively fulfilling it, you are defining happiness. Happiness has a different taste than any other momentarily pleasure in life.

Remember the day when you succeeded in high school or the day when you received your bachelor's degree. Think of that sense of glory and victory. Such pleasure overshadows all the hard efforts, sweat, tears, and blood that have been exerted during your journey toward success.

Try to celebrate each step in your journey, confirming that you are moving in the right direction.

That's why I always recommend to start your adventure toward freedom with the most viable product you feel that will have a significant impact on the market. This will motivate and inspire you to keep moving on in your journey.

BREAKDOWN LARGE PROJECTS TO SMALL MANAGEABLE ONE

Decomposition is to breakdown a large piece of work (working package) into smaller and smaller activities until you reach a level where you can assign each activity to one person (or to yourself).

The second step after such decomposition is to prioritize such activities and put them in a familiar and logical sequence of events to facilitate the execution.

For example:

When you are working on a project for producing a new fragrance brand. The following random activities should be done:

- Design the package;
- Write a business case study for the project;
- develop a financial model to reflect the economics of the project;
- Collect all required data from the market;
- Select the best perfume essence for your product;
- Gather opinions;

As you can see from the above-mentioned high level, working packages are random, and they should be prioritized in a sequence, which makes the overall execution logical:

1- Collect all required data from the market;
2- Select the best perfume essence for your product;
3- Gather opinions;
4- Writing a business case study for the Project;
5- Develop a financial model;
6- Design the package.

They term this in project management as Work Breakdown Structure or "WBS."

In such a sense, you will measure the achievement done in your project, and you can measure it as has been explained previously using the **SPI** and the **CPI** concepts.

Divide your big goal into a set of small executable subgoals and see how beautiful this tip is in action.

I remember one of my old friends who has long been dreaming of living in a particular country. He tried all things to live there but unfortunately couldn't because he could not live there with his current qualifications.

He met me and started to criticize the circumstances that made him the way he is. I told him, why won't you start preparing? Why won't you browse through the immigration requirements for this country and start fulfilling all these requirements one by one? He told me it is a long journey, and I told him there are no shortcuts. If you are willing to succeed, never rely on shortcuts. As the saying goes, **"the journey is better than the destination."**

I won't tell you how things worked out with this guy. He started studying English, more of his professional education, and applied for accredited examinations, where he succeeded. The irony is that after receiving such qualifications, he got hired in his country with a substantial huge salary that made him forget about living in the other country altogether. Still, he reached his goal by traveling to the country of his dreams for vacations and not for work.

GIVING OFF FOR CHARITY

"The simplest acts of kindness are by far more powerful than a thousand heads bowing in prayer."

Mahatma Gandhi

Maybe it is something hard to comprehend if you are more inclined to the scientific reason behind everything but trust me when I say that giving off for the sake of charity has its magic. People will explain this magic differently according to their backgrounds and religions. Still, all will agree on one truth: giving off for charity will increase your money and make you much more prosperous, happier, and more satisfied.

I realized that such magic is duplicated or magnified when the contributed money goes to the right deserving people. Cannot explain what happens; out of nowhere, what has been given to the deserving people returns to me multiplied by ten and sometimes more.

SEARCH FOR PROBLEMS & SOLVE THEM

"The problems are solved, not by giving new information, but by arranging what we have known since long."

Ludwig Wittgenstein

I believe all dictionaries have to put one of the synonyms of the word "problem" as "an opportunity."

Look around you right now; you are surrounded by all kinds of products and services designed and manufactured to solve problems.

Any industry has its problems. Why won't you search for the problems related to your areas of knowledge? If you are an engineer, why won't you think of improving a process or a part of an engine or drawing for a civil structure?

If you are a pharmacist, the doors are wide open for innovation because people suffer from an infinite number of diseases, and they are screaming for someone to relieve their pain.

Bring a piece of paper and a pen and start to write down all the problems that are currently facing you in your daily life. Start from waking up in the morning, drinking your coffee, dressing your clothes, driving your car, etc. I bet you; you will fill the whole paper front and back with countless number of problems.

Remember, it may take one genuine solution to a global problem to make you the next billionaire.

Remember the story of Henry Ford, who provided the average person with an affordable car to ride, and he was the first to implement the assembly line in car manufacturing. He simply introduced a solution to a huge problem: the high price of cars that were not within ordinary people's means.

Remember Bill Gates, who made ordinary people work with computers like geeks without studying sophisticated languages. He simplified the usability of computers, and the world has rewarded him by making him the wealthiest person in the world.

Now you can develop websites, software, and more without knowing a bit of coding. You can design brochures and products without having a bit of official knowledge about design.

These are the products and services that people will be pleased to pay for and spend any sum of money on because they make their lives much more comfortable.

Use lateral thinking to find unorthodox solutions for a given problem. Remember, never sabotage yourself, saying that this has long been a global problem that no one has addressed yet.

 **Lateral Thinking Definition**

Lateral thinking is a manner of solving problems using an indirect and creative approach via reasoning that is not immediately obvious. It involves ideas that may not be obtainable using only traditional step-by-step logic.

Considered pseudo-science by some, the term was first used in 1967 by Edward de Bono in his book **"The Use of Lateral Thinking."** De Bono cites Solomon's Judgment as an example of lateral thinking, where King Solomon resolves a dispute over the parentage of a child by calling for the child to be cut in half and making his judgment according to the reactions that this order receives. Edward de Bono also links lateral thinking with humor, arguing there's a switch-over from a familiar pattern to a new, unexpected one. This moment of surprise generates laughter and unique insight, which facilitates the ability to see a different thought pattern that initially was not obvious. According to de Bono, lateral thinking deliberately distances itself from the standard perception of creativity as "vertical" logic, the classic problem-solving method.

Random Entry Idea Generating Tool:
The thinker chooses a random object or a noun from a dictionary and associates it with the area they are thinking about. De Bono exemplifies this through the randomly-chosen word, "nose," being applied to an office

photocopier, leading to the idea that the copier could produce a lavender smell when it was low on paper.

READ

Perhaps, this is the ultimate quality you need to cultivate in this whole part of the book to provide you with all you need to succeed. If you live for an additional say 100 years ahead, reading will make you live thousands of years more.

Simply put, reading a book gives you the distillation of the wisdom the author has gathered through his or her lifetime, whatever the case might be.

Trust me when I tell you that putting a book together is not an easy task as someone might think. Even if the author of a non-fiction book is not very well known, you must understand that he or she have exerted a lot of effort, distilled a lot of knowledge and experience to compile the manuscript of the book you are holding in your hands.

Hence, reading a book is the shortest cut of understanding an area you want to pioneer. You don't have to fall into the same mistakes others have fallen into.

> "While it is wise to learn from experience, it is wiser to learn from the experiences of others."
>
> Rick Warren

I won't tell you how much money and profits reading has personally provided me or better protected me from losing it.

I remember one rule I have followed all my life if you started reading a book, don't ever put it down until you finish it. This is the best revenge also for boring books. The best revenge is to read it from cover to cover and put it aside forever.

You will benefit anyways; if not from the knowledge found within its pages, you will benefit from something else like, for instance, improving your vocabulary, grammar, fluency in case you are reading out loud like I do.

It is said: "Readers and Leaders." The statement is true; ask any successful person what his number one reason for success is, and I can assure you that he or she will say reading as number one priority. Warren Buffett indicated that the book **"How to win friends and influence people" by Dale Carnegie** had changed his life.

CUSTOMER IS KING

Many employees think that they are earning their living from the salary that is being paid by the employer. Hence, they don't care whether the customer is satisfied or not. An employee's most important thing is to have this monthly paycheck covering his expenses to meet ends.

They don't understand that the company they are working for and the employer who secure their monthly paycheck won't exist without that single customer who is satisfied and is willing to do business with the company again and again.

There are two types of customers, those who didn't do business with you before (let us call them front-end) and those who already did business with you and became devoted to your products or services (let us call them back-end). All successful entrepreneurs confirm that the later (back-end customers) are the most important customers to focus on to succeed.

If you are willing to succeed, you have to treat your customers as kings and never take them for granted. You always have to satisfy them and ask them about their feedback and opinions to make them back-end customers devoted to your brand and products.

VALUE OF TIME

My favorite things in life don't cost any money. It's really clear that the most precious resource we all have is time.
                                                            Steve Jobs

Time is everything. Physicists have agreed to consider it as a fourth dimension, and others confirmed that time is the primary dimension of everything because nothing will exist without it.

While I was younger, I thought that sparring time is something joyful. Playing video games, browsing the internet aimlessly, watching movies, playing cards with friends at the club, and the list is endless. I have realized now that spare time is the place where miracles could happen. This free time is the domain that separates the intelligent, the mediocre, and the stupid.

I also understood that the only thing that could conquer time is speed. For example, If you are late catching a meeting or a necessary appointment, what is the first thing that pops up in your mind? Yes, it is to hurry up; it is to speed up, to recover part of the wasted time.

Albert Einstein confirmed that we could conquer time when we speed up to a level matching the speed of light or faster; at this speed, time becomes no more influential.

I am trying to deliver here that your time is the ultimate precious thing that you should not spare by any means. Never again say I have an hour to kill. Never again doodle aimlessly during a meeting or at home—every single second in your life counts. Sometimes when we are traveling to a beautiful place for a vacation, we just count the days and hours of our stay in such a beautiful place and hope the clock stops ticking to live more in such paradise. Sometimes when we are in love with someone, and we spend time with them, we think the same mentality, and we wish the clock to stop ticking to enjoy some additional minutes with our beloved ones.

Make it a habit to seize every opportunity that you might have of free time and make something useful out of it. You can read, write, and watch a tutorial video about something you want to do (like website designing, for instance). You can call those people who are important to your life like your parents, siblings, relatives, and real friends. But for God's sake, don't spare your time doing nothing.

It is not an invitation here to stop enjoying your time or not to take vacations; on the contrary. What I mean by this section is that you should make the value of every second of your life. If you plan to take a vacation, then take time but make sure that you are enjoying every second of it. Just squeeze the best moments out of it to make use of such an important asset.

	Mr. H. B.

A friend of mine used to trade stocks and currency to earn his living. He told me that he had assigned an excellent and trustworthy broker to perform all trading transactions for him, and he was having a lot of time to spare. He told me that such excessive free time was driving him crazy. He traveled the whole world aimlessly; he camped in different places and still didn't find any satisfaction.

Then he decided to practice Yoga. He was fascinated with yoga and the stories about those people who have practiced it, and it changed their lives forever.

He immediately started his first sessions. After few months of practicing, he told me that he would travel to India with the team to meet with those great trainers and founders who have devised new techniques that provide much comfort and satisfaction to Yoga practitioners.

And behold, H. B. became an international Yoga trainer where people from all walks of life travel to meet him.

He became so and did a successful new business because he invested his spare time in something meaningful. He didn't spare his leisure time aimlessly.

Naïve people think that this is a waste of time, but smart people know very well that although an activity may seem to others as absurd and doesn't make any sense, it could be everything to someone who planned such activity.

Think of thinking. I often got interrupted by people who ask me what's wrong with you because I was just having a moment of silence and reflection. Thinking to them seems like there is something wrong or a waste of time.

As long as you know what you are going to do with your time, I can assure you that you will get the most out of it, and it could pay off a lot of dividends later on during your life.

As Steven R. Covey has stated in his book, **"The seven habits of highly effective people"**: start with the end in mind. Think first of the outcomes of any activity before starting it.

I know a humble office-boy who started to attend English language classes to improve his language. I told him one day, why are you taking these English Courses? He told me to improve my Language. I told him, and why do you want to improve your English Language? He couldn't answer and arrogantly said that he is improving his language for himself, not for anyone else.

Later on, the same office-boy found an excellent work opportunity that required a higher education certificate that he could have had if he had planned for its study instead of aimlessly studying something else.

As the saying goes: "Don't climb the wrong mountain."

I won't tell you how many of us have climbed the wrong mountains during our lifetime. We have befriended the wrong people who have wasted our time and didn't add any value to our lives. We climbed the wrong mountains when we spent a lot of time gaming instead of reading. We climbed the wrong mountains when we got stuck in a career or a job with no future for us. A career that didn't and won't reflect our potentials for success.

We climbed the wrong mountains when we didn't prepare to have our businesses instead of being enslaved to employment.

CLINGING TO LOSS

Sometimes after a lot of persistence and hard work on a product or a project, you realize that the project is no more feasible or the selected product's market is declining (refer to Never Give Up and the 20X Law). In such cases, the best option that you have is an exit plan. You should know that exiting at the right time is a talent exactly matches the skill of selecting the right product or the right market.

An example is the case of blackberry messenger vs. WhatsApp. What happened here is that WhatsApp introduced its messenger that was the easiest to register and the easiest to work with, while blackberry restricted its messenger to the owners of its devices only. In a matter of few months, WhatsApp's usage escalated beyond imagination; people used it for their social and professional lives. Even the blackberry devices' owners wanted to install WhatsApp on their devices.

Blackberry stuck to the competition and did not realize that this is the best time to exit before it is too late. Gradually, blackberry tried to imitate WhatsApp but with no luck. Its messenger was complicated for many people to use, and now the messenger is no more available.

Of course, you can enumerate the analogy of many cases like that Nokia/Microsoft vs. android smartphones.

video cassette vs. CDs/DVDs

Audio Cassette vs. mp3 players/iPod

It is not an invitation to quit with the first obstacle that comes on your way, as we have mentioned in the previous parts; on the contrary, it is an invitation to be smart and know yourself and know your competition and markets. It is the ultimate intelligence to have this sense of intuition that works like a campus for you directing your actions in the right direction at the right time.

There will be some occasions where you will tell yourself I will persist, and I will burn my ships and never retreat, and there will be others where you will compromise for your benefit. You should also know that there are many factors at stake that could change your forecasts and strategies, which you do not influence. Once you realize that such factors have changed your assumptions' fundamentals for the worse, you should reconsider your decisions.

DELAY THE GRATIFICATION

"I slept and dreamt that life was joy. I awoke and saw that life was service. I acted and behold; service was joy."
                                                            Rabindranath Tagore

We all want to be gratified instantaneously. We see that we deserve such gratification and that waiting for it is such a big waste of time. Gratification is those things that make us happy, like marrying the girl of our dreams, like having a lot of money and a lot of associated freedom, the luxury of time to do what we want to do without limitations from employer, family, or anyone.

We are all dreaming of such gratification. Only the wise know very well that you have to work for it to receive such gratification. You have to work and work hard, harder than anyone else, to reach a destination that separates you and the like from others.

When I was young, I used to pass by beautiful rich restaurants and ask myself why only those rich people are visiting such a beautiful place. Then I thought of the idea of equality and how life is unfair. When I grew older, I realized that those who enjoyed this unfair life and wealth had paid the price of such experience by delaying their gratification.

They delayed the gratification of self-esteem and self-respect and went on, knocking on the doors of their customers selling their products with thick skin. They were able to handle brutal rejection from the list of leads they have compiled. They were able to delay wearing expensive clothes and riding luxuries cars, and their friends and family members labeled them as stingy. However, all of them had this common understanding that they will reap the fruits of such delayed gratification sooner or later.

"Sticks and stones may break my bones, But words will never hurt me."

Deciding to study for a Bachelor's Degree, Master's Degree, Ph.D., or to study for a particular certificate like PMP or CFA makes you delay gratification.

You have agreed to delay the gratification of the spare time that you could enjoy watching a movie, playing video games, traveling, or hanging out with your friends at the weekends. However, you have foreseen the results of holding such certificates in your hands and how such acquisition will forever change your life. New opportunities shall open to further position yourself and your family in a completely different social and professional category than the one you are currently staying at.

When you decide to read an important non-fiction book rather than reading a beautiful novel or watching the news, you delayed the gratification for a higher purpose. Maybe, one paragraph written in this book changes your life forever.

When you decide to go to the gym or walk an hour instead of sleeping or relaxing, you delay gratification. However, you know that such activity will sustain your health and the quality of your life. Such a workout will improve your productivity by empowering your immunity and decreasing your illness's chances, and consequently, reducing the time lost in treatment and remedy.

The examples are incalculable, but the idea is the same. There are many trade-offs in front of us every day to decide which one to seize. The choice is always ours to instantly be gratified or delay the same and reap the fruits later.

You would not trust me if I told you that some people cultivate the habit of delayed gratification to the extent that it became their joy instead of the gratification itself. As the saying goes: **"the way is better than the destination."**

TAKE ADVANTAGE OF YOUR APTITUDES

Take a moment and try to think of the millions of unfortunate people who cannot read, write, or even understand English. Millions of others didn't receive a formal education; many live in poverty or are handicapped by malice.

You should know that you have an unfair advantage over those born in least developed and developing countries.

The blessings are enumerable, but what did you do with all of that? Trust me when I say that you have to be grateful for all such blessings and the only way you can express such gratefulness is by doing something tangible.

You should leverage those qualities and gifts, magnifying your powers far beyond your imagination. If you can think, the skies are the limit for your innovation and creativity. If you can read, then you have the experience of others. If you can negotiate a deal with an investor or a bank, you can have unlimited financial resources.

WAKE UP EARLY

"Early Birds get the worm."

I know it might sound hard to comprehend but working early in the morning has its magic pushing you to success. It is like the analogy of a personal computer. When you buy a PC, you experience a snappy and fast performance in the very few days working with it. Unfortunately, the speed and performance slow down step by step after installing many software and stuffing the memory with a lot of "junk," as the saying goes.

The same happens to us; every morning, your human PC is crystal clear, and your mental processors work at their best. You should harness such clarity in innovation or in solving your problems or the problems of others.

Many successful entrepreneurs found their successful business idea during the early mornings while taking a shower, walking their dogs, or commuting to their offices.

Clear thinking and innovation are almost impossible to be done in the context of the day because our brains will be jammed with everyday issues, and quality ideas will be dispersed in the blues.

Try to make it a habit to wake up one hour earlier than every day and dedicate this hour to innovation and entrepreneurship.

In this regard, I would invite you to read a very important book titled **"Deep Work" by Cal Newport.**

THINK BIG

"Once the mind opens to a new idea, it won't return to its original size."

Albert Einstein

Since thinking is thinking, I would instead think big rather than small. Your thoughts and ideas can make a big difference to the people around you and sometimes to the whole world. Don't delimit yourself; don't tell yourself thinking small is simple, but thinking big is complicated.

Trust me when I tell you that sometimes there are elementary and straightforward solutions to big problems, and paradoxically, there are very complicated solutions to small issues.

As we have mentioned before, look for big problems and try to solve them. Trust yourself that you will reach something valuable on your way, searching for a solution for this problem.

One day, one of my friends told me that he is going to China to buy some strange stuff to sell them $1 a piece in the local market. I asked him why you would do that. He told me that's the best that he can do, and the market deserves such cheap stuff.

The problem with this limited thinking is that it leads to nowhere. Even if occasional successes happen, in the end, customers are smart enough to know that they are buying from a flipper.

On the other hand, when you think of significant problems and try to solve them. First, you will have more self-respect that you are after a worthy ideal; second, you will gain the respect of people around you even if your ideas did not materialize. You will always be tagged as the one searching for a solution to this or that big problem, which is a valuable reputation that could support you later on during your success journey.

One of the most critical advantages of thinking big is that it expands your horizons beyond imagination. When you exert your full potential working on a problem worth billions of dollars, you will find yourself at much ease and comfort once you decide to work on other smaller problems worth millions.

The mind is elastic; it can stretch and shrink as the force applied to it. So, always think big to stretch your mind open to a level of intelligence you have never imagined.

I am currently working on a huge problem facing the phosphate industry worldwide, which is called phosphogypsum. This phosphogypsum is a byproduct of the phosphate industry that no one has found a practical use for it, which led all producers to dumb and stack it in vast areas of land. This problem is worth billions of dollars. I have proposed a disruptive solution to this problem to the leading institution in this regard, and I am awaiting their reply. I will share the news regarding this with you on my website. Wish me good luck!

PROTECT YOUR INTELLECTUAL PROPERTY

Will, you may ridicule yourself and say, what I am thinking about and is planning to undertake is not rocket science. You may be true almost 99%, but you don't want to regret the last 1% if it was a real rocket science.

Don't underestimate the power of your thinking, the power of your perception. You may be seeing the world from a completely different perspective than others. Hence you can produce many new and novel ideas that can solve other people's problems and make their lives easier.

Such talent deserves to be protected. It won't be a waste of time or money; on the contrary, it will be a new experience to browse through the process of patent filing and to come in contact with a patent attorney and see the whole process of registration.

Once you have been granted a patent, voilà, you are said to be an inventor. You can put the same on your website, business cards, or where ever you find suitable.

This will boost your reputation a lot and will open a new possibility of cooperation with large companies.

People love smart persons like you; they know very well that they will gain if they cooperate with you.

Hence, before proceeding with any venture, try to think about it for a while. Is it worth to be registered and patented? Will such registration provide me with royalties or a reputation that can further boost my business later on?

If you are going to make a new fragrance recipe out of the already existing one, you don't have to bother yourself with patent filing. But if you are going to lower fuel consumption in the internal combustion engine, you should think million times of registering a patent; who knows, you may sell it to Mercedes or BMW one day.

Caution: Patent filing is expensive, and you will need to hire a professional patent attorney to help you properly file the patent application. If you believe that your intellectual property deserves patent filing, you could approach large investors and negotiate with them a deal. Consider the previously addressed guidelines in this regard (don't forget, NDAs, MOUs, JVs Appendices).

THE IMPORTANCE OF RELATIVE FREEDOM

Generally, if you are relatively free and you are not trapped in the rat race of securing daily necessities, you will end up thinking. Thinking is the only way out.

If you are still an employee, you will probably work 8 to 10 hours a day, which leaves you with 14 to 16 hours. Say you will sleep for 8 hours. Therefore, you are left with 6 to 8 waking hours free. Those few hours are the most critical time if you are willing to change your life for once and forever. In them, you will read, think, innovate, create, and sell. I don't want to repeat myself here, but you should know that you are blessed to have those few hours compared to other struggling fellows who work day and night to meet ends.

PERSISTENCE AND CONSISTENCY

While I am typing these words, I am tempted to work on my second book. If I let such temptations drive me, I will simply lose momentum finishing this current book. That's how plans are ruined. You simply lose momentum.

Sometimes, we are just fed up with the current goal because things didn't materialize to develop the project. Here the word persistence comes into being.

> Your hardest times often lead to the greatest moments of your life. Keep going. Tough situations build strong people in the end."
> Roy T. Bennett

When you set goals for yourself, you have to focus all your efforts, time, resources to finalize this goal. Sometimes, you are obliged to work on some side projects for your life to move on. Still, they have to be always labeled as side projects. It is also an excellent motivator to stay focused on one task you are trying to finish to enjoy executing other important ones.

SPEED UP THE PROCESS

Well, you may have the best ideas in the whole world, and you may have the full potential and capabilities to execute such great ideas, but sluggish execution is the ultimate sin you can do that you may later regret.

If you have a great idea and can execute it, but you procrastinate, others may execute it and reap all the profits being the first one in the market place.

As I have mentioned before, start immediately. Just start putting up the pieces of your project together, piece by piece; you will end up with the first revision of your project, then you can revise and refine something that has a meaning and existence. However, for God's sake, make the process faster. Try to challenge yourself and put some due dates for such projects. An excellent tip is to tell someone you respect and love about such commitment and tell them to track your records.

WHAT MATTERS MOST IN YOUR LIFE?

Maybe this is the most challenging question you will ever encounter if you thought about it for a while.

All of us were raised to conform to a limited number of choices when this question is being presented. Are they health, wealth, or love? Or, maybe the three of them combined. Some people call them the triangle of happiness, and they say if one of the pillars of such a triangle is not there, the others will collapse.

I agree a hundred percent with the three pillars of happiness mentioned above. That's why I have to evaluate every action I make daily against those three pillars. I just ask myself, would so and so advance me toward health, wealth, or love? Does working as an employee, almost 10 hours daily, will contribute to my wealth? Does acquiring an MBA certificate do the same?

Maybe holding more certificates will increase the chances of being hired in better positions with better salaries, but the question is, will this amount to real wealth? We are talking here about this kind of wealth that lets you drive a brand new Lamborghini diablo.

Don't delimit yourself and make the happiness triangle the star that guides you toward your ultimate goals.

THE POWER OF HABITS

"We make our habits; then our habits make us."

Charles C. Noble

Habits are the actions that you do consistently each day that could positively or negatively impact your whole future life.

The problem with habits is that you cannot recognize their impact instantly. For example, if you smoke your first cigarette today, you probably won't contract lung or heart disease. Still, when you develop the habit of smoking and keep doing so for years, at a breaking point, you will face unusual complications that may threaten your life medically.

The same goes for bad eating habits, laziness, putting yourself under stress and pressure consistently, not paying much care to your family or friends. All the previously mentioned are like time bombs; no one knows when they shall explode.

On the other hand, if you developed good habits, they will pay many dividends in the future also at breaking points when you least expect an outcome from such practices.

For example, if you started studying a new language now, after 1 hour, you won't feel much progress in becoming a fluent speaker of such language. Still, after studying the language for many hours daily, one day, you will find yourself talking, reading, writing, and conversing with natives of the language without any problem.

The same goes for working out, reading, writing, meditating, paying some love, and care to your family, asking for friends.

Remember, to cultivate a good habit, you should always think from the inside out. Think about who you want to become rather than what you want to achieve. For example, don't think of discovering new scientific advancements rather than think of being a real scientist. In that sense, you will behave today as a scientist. You will start reading science, listening to lessons, communicating with colleagues and interested parties in the subject, and one day, Hooray, you became a scientist.

The same goes for bodybuilding. Don't say to yourself; I want to build big muscles. Instead, tell yourself I am a bodybuilder; accordingly, you will act like a bodybuilder, you will consistently cultivate the habit of training until one day, Hooray, you are Mr. Olympia.

Someone asked a wise man, "how can you move a mountain? He told him, one stone at a time". That's the essence of habits. You must believe and understand that what you will cultivate today, whether positive or negative, will pay off or fire back shortly. That's why you should choose your habits carefully.

FEAR OF FAILURE

"The real test is not whether you avoid this failure because you won't. It's whether you let it harden or shame you into inaction, or whether you learn from it; whether you choose to persevere."

Barack Obama

I am amazed at the number of people reciting stories about their failure in one endeavor that led them to live as employees for the rest of their lives. Only a few people who say, "After failing in this, I started that, then things begin to change."

If all people are quite sure of their success starting a business, you won't see any employee working at the office. Only those people who accept to fail and learn from such failure are the one who succeed eventually.

Just consider failure as the school fees that you are paying to receive the proper education needed for success.

EDUCATION

"The only skill that will be important in the 21st century is the skill of learning new skills. Everything else will become obsolete over time."

Peter Drucker

We went to school, then to college to be knowledgeable of science, technology, engineering, math, history, literature, business, and the like. We didn't go to these delightful places to be a cog in the gear of employment or to let someone dictate on us what we should do or what we shouldn't.

Education is power. If you can read and write, you have all what it takes to be one of the most powerful creatures walking the earth right now. You can think, modify, create, innovate. You can put your arguments together.

When I meet someone who is misfortunate for not receiving proper education, I thank God for giving me such a blessing. Still, we have to keep in mind that the only way to thank God for such a gift is to put it into use and learn something new every day.

If you cultivated the habit mentioned above, you would link unrelated things together, which is the essence of innovation and creativity.

All innovative ideas were discovered and invented by multi-disciplined chemists or engineers who could link one industry with another, leading to novelty. That's why readers are leaders because they let their minds open by reading different authors' work who have different mindsets.

FOCUS YOUR GOALS

"Concentrate all your thoughts upon the work in hand. The sun's rays do not burn until brought to a focus."
                                                          Alexander Graham Bell

Did you hear about the 5/25 rule before?

The idea is simple; think and write down a long list of all your goals and wishes that you want to fulfill in your lifetime, then choose the most critical five goals out of this long list. The five goals have to be verified again by yourself to make sure that you have selected the right ones. Once you are done, strikeout the other 20 wishes because they are only time wasters.

A couple of days ago, I met an ambitious young engineer who told me that he is preparing for a master's degree in risk management. I told him that he is moving in the right direction to increase his chances of joining multinational corporations.

I met the same guy afterward to hear from him that he is preparing himself to study **MBA** and **PMP** while he desires to study the German language and some French.

The problem with the way of thinking mentioned above is that the guy will achieve nothing; he won't be even a generalist.

Hence, it is advisable to list your goals, make sure that they are real achievable goals, prioritize them, and start pursuing them with all your power. That's the right recipe for success.

NEVER GIVE UP

"Winners are not those who never fail, but those who never quit."

Edwin Louis Cole

The study of most of the world-class entrepreneurs' biographies confirms that those successful people didn't prevail on their first attempt. Even young entrepreneurs have failed several times before they hit the superstar venture that transformed their lives.

Here is a rule that you have to consider before thinking of giving up; it is called the 20X law. It states that you have to do your best in twenty different business endeavors before you feel that you lack something or consider leading a different path toward your success.

Someone may think that twenty is an exaggerated number and that who fails twenty consecutive times is a loser. Most people don't understand that persistence in such an attitude will force the universe to compensate you with success.

CONCLUSION

Starting a business is not rocket science. It is not restricted to the lucky, fortunate minority who happened to have all the success factors play in their favor. Together, we have explored a new approach to generate countless product ideas that could be efficiently executed following the book's guidelines.

The secret of success is to execute. You should simplify the process as much as possible and focus your efforts on selling your successful product. Sales is your career and the career of every successful entrepreneur.

Sell with passion and train your sales force to sell with the same attitude. Treat your customers as queens and kings, and the sky will be the limit for your success.

Thank you for reading this book. I hope it will guide you toward your happiness, success, and fulfillment.

Don't forget to leave a review.

To your success;

Mohamed Kamar

RECOMMENDED READINGS
- How to Win Friends and Influence People by Dale Carnegie;
- The Greatest Salesman In the World by Og Mandino;
- Rich Dad Cashflow Quadrant by Robert Kiyosaki;
- E-myth Mastery by Michael E. Gerber;
- Ready, Fire, Aim by Michael Masterson;
- The Richest Man in Babylon by George Samuel Clason;
- The Tipping Point by Malcolm Gladwell;
- The Millionaire Next Door: The Surprising Secrets of America's Wealthy by Thomas J. Stanley;
- Greatest Discovery by Earl Nightingale;
- Super Thinking: The Big Book of Mental Models by Gabriel Weinberg and Lauren McCann;
- Blue Ocean Strategy by Renée Mauborgne and W. Chan Kim;
- Who Moved My Cheese? by Spencer Johnson;
- Deep Work by Cal Newport;
- Think and Grow Rich by Napoleon Hill;
- How to stop worrying and start living by Dale Carnegie.

APPENDIX 1
"Non-Disclosure Agreement Template"

NON-DISCLOSURE AGREEMENT

This Non-Disclosure and Confidentiality Agreement (this "Agreement") is entered into as of _____, 20____ by and between _____, as a(n) ☐ Individual ☐ Business Entity ("Disclosing Party") and _____, as a(n) ☐ Individual ☐ Business Entity ("Receiving Party").

Disclosing Party and Receiving Party have indicated an interest in exploring a potential business relationship relating to:

_____
_____
_____
_____
_____ (the "Transaction").

In connection with the parties' respective evaluation of the Transaction, each party, their respective affiliates and their respective directors, officers, employees, agents or advisors (collectively, "Representatives") may provide or grant access to certain confidential and proprietary information. A party disclosing its Confidential Information to the other party is hereafter referred to as a "Disclosing Party." A party receiving the Confidential Information of a Disclosing Party is hereafter referred to as a "Receiving Party." In consideration for being furnished Confidential Information, Disclosing Party and Receiving Party agree as follows:

1. Confidential Information. The term "Confidential Information" as used in this Agreement shall mean any data or information that is competitively sensitive material and not generally known to the public, including, but not limited to, information relating to any of the following:

- ☒ product development and plans
- ☐ proprietary concepts
- ☐ technical or product documentation
- ☐ marketing strategies
- ☐ financial development plans
- ☐ operations
- ☐ systems
- ☐ reports

- ☐ specifications
- ☐ computer software
- ☐ source code
- ☐ object code
- ☐ flow charts
- ☐ databases
- ☐ inventions
- ☐ know-how
- ☐ trade secrets
- ☐ customer lists
- ☐ customer relationships
- ☐ customer profiles
- ☐ supplier lists
- ☐ supplier relationships
- ☐ supplier profiles
- ☐ pricing
- ☐ sales estimates
- ☐ business plans and internal

performance results relating to the past

☐ present or future business activities

☐ technical information

☐ design

☐ technical processes

☐ company procedures

☐ formula

☐ improvement

☐ technical or product data

☐ other: _____

_____

which Disclosing Party considers confidential.

2. Exclusions from Confidential Information. The obligation of confidentiality with respect to Confidential Information will not apply to any information:

a. If the information is or becomes publicly known and available other than as a result of prior unauthorized disclosure by Receiving Party or any of its Representatives;

b. If the information is or was received by Receiving Party from a third-party source which, to the best knowledge of Receiving Party or its Representatives, is or was not under a confidentiality obligation to Disclosing Party with regard to such information;

c. If the information is disclosed by Receiving Party with the Disclosing Party's prior written permission and approval;

d. If the information is independently developed by Receiving Party prior to disclosure by Disclosing Party and without the use and benefit of any of the Disclosing Party's Confidential Information; or

e. If Receiving Party or any of its Representatives is legally compelled by applicable law, by any court, governmental agency or regulatory authority or by subpoena or discovery request in pending litigation but only if, to the extent lawful, Receiving Party or its Representatives give prompt written notice of that fact to Disclosing Party prior to disclosure so that Disclosing Party may request a protective order or other remedy to prevent or limit such disclosure and in the absence of such protective order or other remedy, Receiving Party or its Representatives may disclose only such portion of the Confidential Information which it is legally obligated to disclose.

3. **Obligation to Maintain Confidentiality.** With respect to Confidential Information:

a. Receiving Party and its Representatives agree to retain the Confidential Information of the Disclosing Party in strict confidence, to protect the security, integrity and confidentiality of such information and to not permit unauthorized access to or unauthorized use, disclosure, publication or dissemination of Confidential Information except in conformity with this Agreement;

b. Receiving Party and its Representatives shall adopt and/or maintain security processes and procedures to safeguard the confidentiality of all Confidential Information received by Disclosing Party using a reasonable degree of care, but not less than that degree of care used in safeguarding its own similar information or material;

c. Upon the termination of this Agreement, Receiving Party will ensure that all documents, memoranda, notes and other writings or electronic records prepared by it that include or reflect any Confidential Information are returned or destroyed as directed by Disclosing Party;

d. If there is an unauthorized disclosure or loss of any of the Confidential Information by Receiving Party or any of its Representatives, Receiving Party will promptly, at its own expense, notify Disclosing Party in writing and take all actions as may be necessary or reasonably requested by Disclosing Party to minimize any damage to the Disclosing Party or a third party as a result of the disclosure or loss; and

e. (Check one)

☐ Maintain Confidentiality Indefinitely. The obligation not to disclose Confidential Information shall survive the termination of this Agreement, and at no time will Receiving Party or any of its Representatives be permitted to disclose Confidential Information, except to the extent that such Confidential Information is excluded from the obligations of confidentiality under this Agreement pursuant to Paragraph 2 above.

☐ Maintain Confidentiality for a Definite Period. The obligation not to disclose Confidential Information shall remain in effect until _____ ☐ months ☐ years from the date hereof or until the Confidential Information ceases to be a trade secret, except to the extent that such Confidential Information is excluded from the obligations of confidentiality under this Agreement pursuant to Paragraph 2 above.

4. Non-Disclosure of Transaction. Without Disclosing Party's prior written consent, neither Receiving Party nor its Representatives shall disclose to any other person, except to the extent, the provisions of Paragraph 2 apply: (a) the fact that Confidential Information has been made available to it or that it has inspected any portion of the Confidential Information; (b) the fact that the Disclosing Party and Receiving Party are having discussions or negotiation concerning the Transaction; or (c) any of the terms, conditions or other facts with respect to the Transaction.

5. Non-Compete. (INITIAL if you want to include this clause. CROSS OUT if you do not.)

_____ Receiving Party agrees that at no time will Receiving Party engage in any business activity which is competitive with Disclosing Party, nor work for any company which competes with Disclosing party:

☐ During the term of Receiving Party's relationship with Disclosing Party.

☐ From the date of this Agreement until _____, 20____.

6. Non-Solicitation. (INITIAL if you want to include this clause. CROSS OUT if you do not.)

_____ Receiving Party agrees to not solicit any employee or independent contractor of Disclosing Party on behalf of any other business enterprise, nor shall Receiving Party induce any employee or independent contractor associated with Disclosing Party to terminate or breach an employment, contractual or other relationship with Disclosing Party:

☐ During the term of Receiving Party's relationship with Disclosing Party.

☐ From the date of this Agreement until _____, 20____.

7. Representatives. Receiving Party will take reasonable steps to ensure that its Representatives adhere to the terms of this Agreement. Receiving Party will be responsible for any breach of this Agreement by any of its Representatives.

8. Disclaimer. There is no representation or warranty, express or implied, made by Disclosing Party as to the accuracy or completeness of any of its Confidential Information. Except for the matters set forth in this Agreement, neither party will be under any obligation with regard to the Transaction. Either party may, in its sole discretion: (a) reject any proposals made by the other party or its Representatives with respect to the Transaction; (b) terminate discussions and negotiations with the other party or its Representatives at any time and for any reason or for no reason; and (c) change the procedures relating to the consideration of the Transaction at any time without prior notice to the other party.

9. Remedies. Each party agrees that use or disclosure of any Confidential Information in a manner inconsistent with this Agreement will give rise to irreparable injury for which: (a) money damages may not be a sufficient remedy for any breach of this Agreement by such party; (b) the other party may be entitled to specific performance and injunction and other equitable relief with respect to any such breach; (c) such remedies will not be the exclusive remedies for any such breach, but will be in addition to all other remedies available at law or in equity; and (d) in the event of litigation relating to this Agreement, if a court of competent jurisdiction determines in a final non-appealable order that one party, or any of its Representatives, has breached this Agreement, such party will be liable for reasonable legal fees and expenses incurred by the other party in connection with such litigation, including, but not limited to, any appeals.

10. Notices. All notices given under this Agreement must be in writing. A notice is effective upon receipt and shall be sent via one of the following methods: delivery in person, overnight courier service, certified or registered mail, postage prepaid, return receipt requested, addressed to the party to be notified at the below address or by facsimile at the below facsimile number or in the case of either party, to such other party, address or facsimile number as such party may designate upon reasonable notice to the other party.

Disclosing Party

Name: _____

Representative name:
_____, Title:
_____

Address:
_____
_____

Phone number: _____

Fax number: _____

Receiving Party

Name: _____

Representative name:
_____, Title:
_____

Address:

_____

_____

Phone number: _____

Fax number: _____

11. Termination. This Agreement will terminate on the earlier of:

    (a) the written agreement of the parties to terminate this Agreement;

    (b) the consummation of the Transaction; or

    (c) _____ ☐ months ☐ years from the date hereof.

12. Amendment. This Agreement may be amended or modified only by a written agreement signed by both of the parties.

13. Jurisdiction. This Agreement will be governed by and construed in accordance with the laws of the State of _____, without regard to the principles of conflict of laws. Each party consents to the exclusive jurisdiction of the courts located in the State of _____ for any legal action, suit or proceeding arising out of or in connection with this Agreement. Each party further waives any objection to the laying of venue for any such suit, action or proceeding in such courts.

14. Miscellaneous. This Agreement will inure to the benefit of and be binding on the respective successors and permitted assigns of the parties. Neither party may assign its rights or delegate its duties under this Agreement without the other party's prior written consent. In the event that any provision of this Agreement is held to be invalid, illegal or unenforceable in whole or in part, the remaining provisions shall not be affected and shall continue to be valid, legal and enforceable as though the invalid, illegal or unenforceable parts had not been included in this Agreement. Neither party will be charged with any waiver of any provision of this Agreement, unless such waiver is evidenced by a writing signed by the party and any such waiver will be limited to the terms of such writing.

IN WITNESS WHEREOF, the parties hereto have executed this Agreement as of the date first written above.

Disclosing Party:

Receiving Party:

Source: https://legaltemplates.net/form/non-disclosure-agreement/

APPENDIX 2
"Memorandum of Understanding Template"

MEMORANDUM OF UNDERSTANDING

This Memorandum of Understanding (MOU), hereinafter referred to as the Memorandum, entered into on _____, by and between _____ residing at _____, _____,

_____, hereinafter referred to as the "First Party," and _____ residing at _____, _____,

_____, hereinafter referred to as the "Second Party," and collectively known as the "Parties" for the purpose of establishing and achieving various goals and objective relating to the _____ .

WHEREAS, the Parties above desire to enter into the herein described agreement in which they shall work together to accomplish the goals and objectives set forth;

AND WHEREAS, the Parties are desirous to enter an understanding, thus setting out all necessary working arrangements that both Parties agree shall be necessary to complete this _____;

MISSION

The aforementioned _____ has been established with the following intended mission in mind:

_____

PURPOSE AND SCOPE

The Parties intend for this Memorandum of Understanding to provide the cornerstone and structure for any and all possibly impending binding contract which may be related to the _____.

OBJECTIVES

The Parties shall endeavor to work together to develop and establish policies and procedures that will promote and sustain a market for _____, and intend to maintain a product and/or services that meets or exceeds all business and industry standards.

RESPONSIBILITIES AND OBLIGATIONS OF THE PARTIES

It is the desire, and the wish of the Parties mentioned above to this MOU Agreement that this document should not and thus shall not establish nor create any form or manner of a formal agreement or indenture, but rather an agreement between the Parties to work together in such a way that would promote a genuine atmosphere of collaboration and alliance in support of an effective and efficient partnership and leadership meant to maintain, safeguard and sustain sound and optimal managerial, financial and administrative commitment with regards to all matters related to the _____.

TIMELINE

The above outlined scope and objective shall be contingent on the Parties obtaining the necessary funds required for the _____ as described within any grant or business loan application, if any. Responsibilities under this Memorandum of Understanding may coincide with the grant period.

TERMS OF UNDERSTANDING

The term of this Memorandum of Understanding shall be for a period of _____ from the aforementioned effective date and maybe extended upon written mutual agreement of both Parties.

AMENDMENT OR CANCELLATION OF THIS MEMORANDUM

This Memorandum of Understanding may be amended or modified at any time in writing by both parties' mutual consent.

In addition, the Memorandum of Understanding may be canceled by either party with _____ days advance written notice, with the exception where the cause for cancellation may include, but is not limited to, a material and significant breach of any of the provisions contained herein, when it may be canceled upon delivery of written notice to the other party.

GENERAL PROVISIONS

The Parties acknowledge and understand that they must fulfill their responsibilities under this Memorandum of Understanding, following the law's provisions and regulations that govern their activities. Nothing in the Memorandum is intended to negate or otherwise render ineffective any such provisions or operating procedures. The parties assume full responsibility for their performance under the terms of this Memorandum.

Suppose at any time either party is unable to perform their duties or responsibilities under this Memorandum of Understanding consistent with such party's statutory and regulatory mandates. In that case, the affected party shall immediately provide written notice to the other party to establish a date for resolving the matter.

LIMITATION OF LIABILITY

No rights or limitation of rights shall arise or be assumed between the Parties as a result of the terms of this Memorandum of Understanding.

ARBITRATION/MEDIATION DISPUTE RESOLUTION

The Parties to this Memorandum of Understanding agree that should any dispute arise through any aspect of this relationship, including, but not limited to, any matters, controversies, or claims; the Parties shall confer in good faith promptly resolve any dispute. Suppose the Parties are unable to resolve the issue or dispute between them. In that case, the matter shall be mediated and/or arbitrated in an attempt to resolve any issues between the Parties.

The parties agree that any claim or dispute that arises from for through this agreement, the relationship or obligations contemplated or outlined within this agreement, if not resolved through mediation, shall then go to and be resolved through final and binding arbitration. Any decision reached by the Arbitrator shall be final and binding and, if required, may be entered as a judgment in any court having jurisdiction.

Suppose any court having jurisdiction should determine that any portion of this Agreement is invalid or unenforceable. In that case, only that portion shall be deemed null and not significant, while the balance of this Agreement shall remain in full effect and enforceable. This Agreement shall be interpreted and governed by and following the Federal Arbitration Act 9 U.S.C. §1-16.

NOTICE

Any notice or communication required or permitted under this Memorandum shall be sufficiently given if delivered in person or by certified mail, return receipt requested, the address outlined in the opening paragraph, or to such address as one may have furnished the other in writing.

GOVERNING LAW

This Memorandum of Understanding shall be governed by and construed in accordance with the laws of the State of _____.

SEVERABILITY CLAUSE

If any provision of this Memorandum of Understanding shall be deemed to be severable or invalid, and if any term, condition, phrase or portion of this Memorandum shall be determined to be unlawful or otherwise unenforceable, the remainder of the Memorandum shall remain in full force and effect, so long as the clause severed does not affect the intent of the parties. If a court found that any provision of this Memorandum is invalid or unenforceable, it would become valid and enforceable by limiting said provision. It would become valid and enforceable, then said provision should be deemed to be written, construed, and enforced as so limited.

ASSIGNMENT

Neither party to this Memorandum of Understanding may assign or transfer the responsibilities or agreement made herein without the prior written consent of the non-assigning party, which approval shall not be unreasonably withheld.

ENTIRE UNDERSTANDING

The herein contained Memorandum of Understanding constitutes the Parties' entire understanding about all matters contemplated hereunder at this time. The Parties signing this MOU desire or intend that any implementing contract, license, or other agreement entered into between the Parties subsequent hereto shall supersede and preempt any conflicting provision of this Memorandum of Understanding whether written or oral.

MOU SUMMARIZATION

FURTHERMORE, the Parties to this MOU have mutually acknowledged and agreed to the following:

- The Parties to this MOU shall work together in a cooperative and coordinated effort, and in such a manner and fashion to bring about the achievement and fulfillment of the goals and objectives of this _____.

- It is not the intent of this MOU to restrict the Parties to this Agreement from their involvement or participation with any other public or private individuals, agencies, or organizations.

- The Parties to this MOU shall mutually contribute and take part in any and all phases of the planning and development of this _____, to the fullest extent possible.

- It is not the intent or purpose of this MOU to create any rights, benefits and/or trust responsibilities by or between the parties.

- The MOU shall in no way hold or obligate either Party to supply or transfer funds to maintain and/or sustain the _____.

- Should there be any need or cause for the reimbursement or the contribution of any funds to or in support of the _____, it shall then be controlled in accordance with _____ governing laws, regulations and/or procedures.

- If contributed funds should become necessary, any such endeavor shall be outlined in a separate and mutually agreed upon written agreement by the Parties or representatives of the Parties following current governing laws and regulations. In no way does this MOU provide such right or authority.

- The Parties to this MOU have the right to individually or jointly terminate their participation in this Agreement provided that advanced written notice is delivered to the other party.

- Upon signing this MOU by both Parties, this Agreement shall be in full force and effect.

AUTHORIZATION AND EXECUTION

The signing of this Memorandum of Understanding does not constitute a formal undertaking. As such, it intends merely that the signatories shall strive to reach, to the best of their abilities, the goals and objectives stated in this MOU.

This Agreement shall be signed by _____ and _____ and shall be effective as of the date first written above.

_____   _____
(First Party Signature)   (Date)

_____   _____
_____   _____
(Second Party Signature)   (Date)

APPENDIX 3
"Joint Venture Agreement"

JOINT VENTURE AGREEMENT

This Joint Venture Agreement (this "Agreement") is entered into as of the _____ day of _____, 20_____ (the "Effective Date") by and between _____ [name of entity 1], a _____ [state of entity 1 formation] _____ [type of entity 1: corporation/limited liability company/partnership/limited partnership/limited liability partnership] ("_____") [abbreviated name of entity 1] located at _____ [address of entity 1] and _____ [name of entity 2], a _____ [state of entity 2 formation] _____ [type of entity 2: corporation/limited liability company/partnership/limited partnership/limited liability partnership] ("_____") [abbreviated name of entity 2] located at _____ [address of entity 2].

1. Formation. The parties have indicated an interest in forming and establishing a joint venture for the exclusive purpose of _____ [purpose of joint venture] (the "Joint Venture"). The Joint Venture shall do business under the name _____ [joint venture name], and shall have its principal office and place of business at _____ [legal address] or such other place(s) as shall be designated from time to time.

2. No Partnership. The Joint Venture shall not be construed to create a partnership or any other fiduciary obligations between the parties.

3. Contributions. For the purpose of the Joint Venture, [name of entity 1] shall make an initial capital contribution of _____ [dollar amount/property/other value] and [name of entity 2] shall make an initial capital contribution of _____ [dollar amount/property/other value].

If the Joint Venture requires additional funds, the parties shall make additional contributions in the following proportion: [entity 1] will contribute _____ [additional contributions from entity 1] and [entity 2] will contribute _____ [additional contributions from entity 2]

The parties own the following percentage interest in the Joint Venture: [entity 1] will own _____ [ownership percentage from entity 1] and [entity 2] will own _____ [ownership percentage from entity 2]

4. Distribution of Profits. Net profits and net losses accruing to the Joint Venture shall be held and distributed to the Parties in the following proportion: [entity 1] will receive _____ [proportion of profits entity 1 will each receive] and [entity 2] will receive _____ [proportion of profits entity 2 will each receive]

5. Management. The Manager, Management Committee, or _____ will be responsible for the following duties and obligations of the Joint Venture: (a) managing day to day business affairs; (b) monitoring, controlling and directing the financial, business and operational affairs; (c) properly maintaining account books and financial records according to standard accounting practices; (d) using express or implied authority granted by this Agreement to handling all other issues; and (e) hiring production and administration staff and third party contractors as needed, including any required labor negotiations.

Disagreements. If the parties disagree on a material issue and cannot agree on a mutually satisfactory decision or solution, then a deadlock shall be deemed to have occurred. If a deadlock occurs, the parties accept and understand that they will engage in [a buy-out/mediation/arbitration/state other remedy].

In a buy-out, one party (the "Offeror") may offer to purchase the Joint Venture interest of the other party (the "Offeree") by notifying the Offeree in writing of an irrevocable offer to purchase. The Offeree shall then have the right to either buy the interest of the Offeror at the designated price and terms or sale its own interest at the designated price and terms for _____ (#) days.

6. No Exclusivity. This Agreement does not obligate either party to conduct business exclusively with the other party.

7. **Confidentiality.**

a. **Confidential and Proprietary Information.** In the course of the Joint Venture, the parties will be exposed to confidential and proprietary information. Confidential and proprietary information shall mean any data or information that is competitively sensitive material and not generally known to the public, including, but not limited to, information relating to development and plans, marketing strategies, finance, operations, systems, proprietary concepts, documentation, reports, data, specifications, computer software, source code, object code, flow charts, data, databases, inventions, know-how, trade secrets, customer lists, customer relationships, customer profiles, supplier lists, supplier relationships, supplier profiles, pricing, sales estimates, business plans and internal performance results relating to the past, present or future business activities, technical information, design, process, procedure, formula, or improvement, which the the parties consider confidential and proprietary. The parties acknowledge and agree that the confidential and proprietary information is valuable property, developed over a long period of time at substantial expense and that it is worthy of protection.

b. **Confidentiality Obligations.** Except as otherwise expressly permitted in this Agreement, the parties shall not disclose or use in any manner, directly or indirectly, any confidential and proprietary information either during the term of this Agreement or at any time thereafter, except as required to perform their duties and responsibilities or with the other party's prior written consent. Both parties agree that all confidential and proprietary information disclosed and received shall not remain secret and confidential during the Term of this Agreement and continue thereafter for __[written number of years]____ ([#]) years after the Agreement is terminated or expires.

c. **Rights in Confidential and Proprietary Information.** All ideas, concepts, work product, information, written material or other confidential and proprietary information disclosed to either party (i) are and shall remain the sole and exclusive property of the disclosing party, and (ii) are disclosed or permitted to be acquired by the receiving party solely in reliance on this Agreement to maintain them in confidence and not to use or disclose them to any other person except in furtherance of the Joint Venture. Except as expressly provided herein, this Agreement does not confer any right, license, ownership or other interest or title in, to or under the confidential and proprietary information to the receiving party.

d. **Irreparable Harm.** Employee acknowledges that use or disclosure of any confidential and proprietary information in a manner inconsistent with this Agreement will give rise to irreparable injury for which damages would not be an adequate remedy. Accordingly, in addition to any other legal remedies which may be available at law or in equity, the Company shall be entitled to equitable or injunctive relief against the unauthorized use or disclosure of confidential and proprietary information. The Company shall be entitled to pursue any other legally permissible remedy available as a result of such breach, including but not limited to damages, both direct and consequential. In any action brought by the Company under this Section, the

Company shall be entitled to recover its attorney's fees and costs from Employee.

8. **Notices.** All notices given under this Agreement must be in writing. A notice is effective upon receipt and shall be sent via one of the following methods: delivery in person, overnight courier service, certified or registered mail, postage prepaid, return receipt requested, addressed to the party to be notified at the below address or by facsimile at the below facsimile number or in the case of either party, to such other party, address or facsimile number as such party may designate upon reasonable notice to the other party.

[Name of Entity/Individual 1]

[Name of Contact Person and Title, if Entity]

[Street Address]

[City, State, Zip Code]

[Telephone Number]

[Facsimile Number]

[Name of Entity/Individual 2]

[Name of Contact Person and Title, if Entity]

[Street Address]

[City, State, Zip Code]

[Telephone Number]

[Facsimile Number]

9. **Termination.** This Agreement will terminate on the earlier of: (a) the written agreement of the parties to terminate this Agreement; (b) the consummation of the Joint Venture; (c) _____ [period of time: e.g. six months, one year, two years] from the date hereof; or (d) the completion of the following objective: _____ [describe dissolution event, completion of a project, goal, or change in market conditions].

10. **Amendment.** This Agreement may be amended or modified only by a written agreement signed by both of the parties.

11. **Jurisdiction.** This Agreement will be governed by and construed in accordance with the laws of the State of _____, without regard to the principles of conflict of laws. Each party consents to the exclusive jurisdiction of the courts located in the State of _____ for any legal action, suit or proceeding arising out of or in connection with this Agreement. Each party further waives any objection to the laying of venue for any such suit, action or proceeding in such courts.

12. **Miscellaneous.** This Agreement will inure to the benefit of and be binding on the respective successors and permitted assigns of the parties. Neither party may assign its rights or delegate its duties under this Agreement without the

other party's prior written consent. No consent shall be required if the assignment or transfer is pursuant to a sale of all or substantially all of a party's assets or business, but written consent must be given within _____ days of such assignment or transfer. In the event that any provision of this Agreement is held to be invalid, illegal or unenforceable in whole or in part, the remaining provisions shall not be affected and shall continue to be valid, legal and enforceable as though the invalid, illegal or unenforceable parts had not been included in this Agreement. Neither party will be charged with any waiver of any provision of this Agreement, unless such waiver is evidenced by a writing signed by the party and any such waiver will be limited to the terms of such writing.

IN WITNESS WHEREOF, the parties hereto have executed this Agreement as of the date first written above.

[Name of Entity/Individual 1]

By: _____

Name: _____

Title: _____

[Name of Entity/Individual 2]

By: _____

Name: _____

Title: _____

APPENDIX 4
"Business Plan Guidelines"

Table of Contents

Executive Summary
- Summary
- Management Team
- Products and Services
- Customers
- Marketing and Sales
- Financial Forecast
- Required Funds

Company and Financing
- Company Overview
- Management Team
- Required Funds
- Exit Strategy
- Mission Statement
- Company History
- Locations and Facilities
- Products and Services

Products and Services
- Competitors
- Sourcing and Fulfillment
- Technology

- Intellectual Property
- Future Products and Services

Customers
- Market Overview
- Market Needs
- Market Trends
- Market Growth
- Industry Analysis
- Key Customers

Marketing and Sales
- Overview
- Positioning
- Pricing
- Promotion
- Distribution

Strategy and Implementation
- Milestones
- SWOT Analysis
- Competitive Edge
- Strategic Alliances

Financial Plan
- Sales Forecast

    Personnel Plan

    Budget

    Cash Flow Assumptions

    Loans and Investments

    Starting Balances

    Historical Financials

    Key Metrics for Success

Financial Statements

    Profit and Loss Statement Table

    Balance Sheet Table

    Cash Flow Statement Table

    Financial Ratio Table

Appendix

    Sales Forecast

    Personnel Plan

    Budget

    Loans and Investments

    Profit and Loss Statement

    Balance Sheet

    Cash Flow Statement

Glossary

Source: https://legaltemplates.net/form/business-plan-template/

www.ingramcontent.com/pod-product-compliance
Lightning Source LLC
Chambersburg PA
CBHW072027230526
45466CB00020B/1020